THE MILITANT HACKWRITER

The Militant Hackwriter

FRENCH POPULAR LITERATURE 1800 — 1848
ITS INFLUENCE, ARTISTIC AND POLITICAL

by

LUCIAN W. MINOR

Bowling Green University Popular Press
Bowling Green, Ohio 43403

Library of Congress Card Catalog Number 75-524

ISBN: 0-87972-105-7 Clothbound
       0-87972-106-5 Paperback

TO VERA

For the best of all reasons

PREFACE

The present book had its inception when years ago, as an unruly graduate student, I grew angry over the way manuals of French literature seemed to schematize its development in the 19th century. The straight, teleological lines they drew from great author to great author did not seem to match the twists and turns I saw in the novel and the drama as they changed over the decades. There must, my rebellion argued, be more than that. And, of course, there was.

But there would not have been opportunity to set down even a part of it without the kindness of several administrative officers, colleagues and valued friends. The State University College at Fredonia granted me sabbatical leave in which to read and consider. The Research Foundation of the State University of New York helped materially in allowing me to bring the project to conclusion. I express here my lively appreciation for their support.

Encouragement to quell doubts, a rigorous critical judgment and a vast knowledge were the freely given gifts of an already deeply valued friend. I gladly voice my warmest appreciation to Professor William Neville of this college for his unstinting help. Professor Douglas Shepard also of this college gave generously of his time and finely honed skills in reviewing the manuscript. I offer him my admiring thanks. Finally, Professor Vera Lee of Boston College gave me her loving encouragement, unflagging support, her skilled critiques and her busy red pencil. I offer her what can only be partial repayment: my profound gratitude and the dedication of this volume.

Fredonia, N. Y.
March, 1974

TABLE OF CONTENTS

Chapter

INTRODUCTION

↣   *WHILE LOUIS XVIII, CHARLES X AND LOUIS PHILIPPE*
ruled in France, a vast majority of politically unenfranchised Frenchmen were developing their own subculture. Only recently literate, they fashioned their own
literature. It consisted of two important genres: the
popular novel and the melodrama. As we trace these
genres from the turn of the nineteenth century until
that moment of February 25, 1848, when the Second
Republic was declared, we are also led to a detailed
scrutiny of the injustices which the immense majority
of the French suffered and of the political causes they
espoused. The succession of heroes and villains in their
literature mirrored accurately the fears and hopes they
felt.

Literary historians have been less attentive than
they ought to have been in assessing the importance
and influence of this subculture. Although they have
indeed followed the evolution of France's well-bred
literature, have done proper honor to the literary

1

"greats," they have nonetheless given very little thought to the existence, much less the role, of the popular literature. Where they have treated popular writers, it was done less to consider or analyse the works themselves but rather to aid critics in explaining away small uncertainties about the writings of the honored writers. When one spoke of roses, one might have occasion briefly to consider the fertilizer, but the important thing was the elegant plant itself.

The following pages speak precisely of this literary subculture as fertilizer. They treat the French people and their literature. They trace its beginnings, show its rapid growth and demonstrate its decisive but largely unrecognized influence upon the respectable literature.

In the well-bred novel, a hero suffered, superior, alone and totally immersed in himself. But the popular novel's hero was a quite different sort. He was of the lower classes, energetic, little given to moody introspection and philosophically untroubled as he pursued his goals. He had a living to earn, a young girl to court and problems that everyone could understand.

As for melodrama, popular and crude, it made use of techniques and plots that the respectable theaters scorned. Far from focusing upon the dilemma of a princess whose brother must, in defense of family honor, slay her fiancé, the melodrama brought sobs to its uneducated audiences when it pictured the much more plebian problems of poverty, sickness, lost life savings, gambling, bastardy and orphanhood.

It is precisely this detailing of life among the unlettered and unhonored majority of the French that distinguishes the popular literature. Significantly, by

1848, all of French literature seemed to be following this same path.

But the influence of the popular novel and theater did not restrict itself to the purely literary. It had, as well, a profound effect upon the whole of French political and social life. The humanitarian, democratic and even socialist turn which French fiction took as the century neared the midpoint was vitally important in the creation of the Second Republic as well as in the truly revolutionary legislature it voted into being. Already contemporaneous, the popular literature became politicized and began both to demonstrate the ills of the masses and to propose solutions for them. Much of the social legislation grudgingly voted by the Second Republic had first been resolutely proposed and popularized in cheap novels and melodramas.

The growth of realism in literature and in French political life: these were the portentous contributions of popular literature. By 1848 the great majority had breached the barriers, and neither French literature nor French political life would ever be the same. The popular literature, like Hugo's *Ruy Blas,* was to prove that it was "une force qui va."

CHAPTER I

Of Oligarchies, Political and Literary

→→ *JEDEDIAH CLEISHBOTHAM IS AN ODD NAME; BUT THAT IS* the name by which cultivated French readers first came to know Walter Scott. His *Guy Mannering* bore that unprepossessing pseudonym when it first appeared in translation, in 1816. The genteel reading public slowly began to fall in love with Cleishbotham-Scott, and by 1820 the conquest was complete. Over the next twenty years they devoured his novels. They read, raved over and tried to copy his marvellous ways with the historical romance.

Nothing could have been more enchanting to the well mannered than his damsels, fair youths, lute-playing minstrels, chatelaines with long tresses, towers, dungeons and crenelated battlements. But while well-bred French folk read Scott and dreamed their dreams, another sort of literature seized and held its own quite different audience. The popular novel was created for and read by the newly literate masses of French, the unrefined, uneducated and, in the main, unwashed. Their preferences had little in common with the civilized passion for the Waverly novels. Theirs was a taste for strong primary flavors, not overly imaginative, and lacking the experience to distinguish subtleties.

The same differences in taste also separated the cultured theater from that of the people. In the respectable theater, playwrights tried to revive the honored French tradition. But the time was no more when pale shades of classical heroines could move audiences greatly; princesses' passions à la Racine were no longer in season. The Théâtre Français and other fashionable houses tried to mine the classical vein but earned only dutiful applause from a shrinking audience. At the same time, in cheaper, cruder halls far from the elegant niceties of loge seat and rich red velvet, the popular theater was energetically seeking and holding its own audience of the poorer classes of Parisian workers.

The lending libraries that dotted French cities and towns even in the remotest provinces illustrated the most immediate distinction between the two literatures. The would-be borrower of a novel had no more than set foot in the library when he saw upon the shelves two easily distinct groups of books. One contained rather large, well-bound volumes of octavo format (about six by nine and a-half inches). These were the genteel novels, published usually in two or three volumes. Other shelves held smaller, less impressive duodecimo novels (about five by seven and three-quarters inches), published usually in four or even as many as eight volumes. These, of course, were the popular novels.

Nor had a theatergoer any trouble telling what sort of play he would see, simply from the address of the theater itself. The popular halls were grouped in the older, poorer section of Paris, where the working class lived. But the Théâtre Français raised its small, elegant façade in the very center of the Palais-Royal, between the magnificent mansion that Mazarin had built and the starkly impressive buildings that constitute the enclave of the Louvre. With this sort of dramatic segregation, even a provincial bumpkin would have known the difference.

These external differences separating the refined from the crude were small, however, compared to internal ones, particularly in content. The typical French Restoration novel of manners was routine in plot and more than a little insipid. The reader was offered a fare of tales bearing elegantly indolent female titles—*Corinne, Caroline, Delphine*—written by cultured ladies and, laughably, by male imitators hiding behind feminine pennames. But gender of author notwithstanding, the product was repetitious and all too dated. Décor, milieu and daily life, all were omitted to leave room for the description of "fatal passions" that consumed "souls of fire," halfway between eighteenth-century sentimentalism and the emotional storms of romanticism. Like a somewhat faded brocade in a once successful pattern, these refined novels were competently made, but they had become pallid with age.

The popular novel came as a boisterously effective antidote. Daily life, with its earthy décor, appeared noisily and messily in the story. Verisimilitude and psychological accuracy asked for their gloves and fled the unseemliness of stories describing common people in common settings but behaving astonishingly. Even though a mere peasant or doorman, the hero of these rough novels always fell in love instantly, possessed the courage of a lion and was unfailingly kind to old ladies. His beloved heroine embodied youth, shy innocence and a troubling abundance of physical charms. Invariably, after the required number of narrow escapes from burning farmhouses, abductions by evil countesses or hired heavies, the two were united in eager connubial bliss and, the reader was encouraged to assume, lived happily ever after.

Divisions between the dramas of the two literatures were every bit as great. Where the leisurely, well-bred theater took five acts of rimed alexandrines to dissect the dilemma of a noblewoman whose brother was honor bound to kill her fiancé, the popular drama was more direct. It needed only three acts to solve the problem of a young country girl who could not marry her sturdy suitor until the secret of her birth and her suspected bastardy had been cleared away. This was the theater working men and women attended, to sob, smile, and cheer, melodrama crude, in prose, but always ending happily.

The French novel too had a long and carefully tended inheritance. For centuries grammarians and critics had honed and polished its prose. It was only natural that well-educated French people should judge acutely and prize highly an impeccably turned piece of work and be incisively severe with lapses from their standards. The readers of the popular novels were not so demanding. Lacking the education, the standards by which to judge, they took a much more direct pleasure in their reading. They wanted a story and were not disposed to be unduly critical about the style of telling. In essence, the relation between the crude literature and the civilized was that of an oligarchy. The wealthy and educated exercised cultural rule over the respectable novel and drama but were almost unaware if not totally ignorant of the popular literature.

The ignorance of one another which the cultured and uneducated classes shared in the field of literature sprang from a much wider, much more fundamental separation, one organic to the political structure. Here the division was almost total. Little in the monarchy, as restored by the allies after Waterloo, gave indication that there existed, in any real or important sense, a French population below the bourgeoisie. Far exceeding the literary, the political oligarchy was well nigh all encompassing, quite deliberately and watchfully maintained. Embodied in law and royal decree, it was enforced by the courts, the police and, when necessary, the army.

During the whole of the Restoration, France was governed determinedly by a small fraction of the upper classes, about one three-hundredth of the population. Its control of the country was scarcely challenged. Louis XVIII reigned—but à l'anglaise: in a limited monarchy, aided in his decisions by a legislature. King ruled; oligarchy controlled. Although the privileged classes argued bitterly as they governed, they found comforting agreement in literature; they found confirmation of their own ideas and agreeable flattery in Scott's burnishing of noble escutcheons. The returned nobility longed to restore the prestige of the warrior class to which they belonged. Scott's novels glorified feudal ideas of homage, noble courage and fealty to king. In this way they carried not only an enchanting story but also strong political reaffirmation. The newly restored Bourbon court could only benefit from these romances.

Earlier, under Napoleon, both literature and fashion had made heavy use of classical Roman forms. Women's clothing had affected the modes of patrician Rome while drama showed republican Romans in examples of outstanding civic virtue. But reminders of pagan Rome raised unfortunate thoughts about the assassination of Caesar. Such allusions could not possibly be relished by the restored monarchy. After all, Louis XVI and Marie Antoinette had died at the guillotine. A Christian kingdom required a fashion in literature more in keeping with the metaphysics of monarchy to celebrate the timelessness of the Bourbon contribution to France. Then Walter Scott appeared. This skillful novelist painted king, court and knighthood in a romantic mold. What was more, he seemed unmistakably a royalist himself. When French royalists discovered that he had even written a pamphlet against Bonaparte, their joy was complete. Straightaway, their favorite novelist became "the poet of the legitimacy" of monarchy as well. French imitators of Scott sensed the new wind and got furiously to work.

Balzac, newly arrived in Paris, worked hard if clumsily to produce a novel "in the manner" of Scott. His *Clothilde de Lusignan* earned the quick failure it deserved. The young royalist, Hugo, added his own efforts to the swell of imitations. In his *Han d'Islande* Hugo changed the locale from Scotland to the icy northlands which had long fascinated the French imagination, but he generally stuck to Scott's pattern. No one reads

the novel today, but Vigny read it then and wrote Hugo
in grandiloquent praise.

> It is a fine and great and lasting work you have
> done . . . you have laid the foundations of
> Walter Scott in France . . . all the interest is
> there, everything is vibrant . . . I thank you
> in the name of France.[1]

Such flattering thanks from the noble Vigny must
have warmed Hugo's ambitious royalist heart. In fact,
Vigny was doubtless more approving of the novel's noble
sentiments than of its qualities as fiction. In any case,
the compliment was neatly turned, as such niceties from
a nobleman should be.

The rest of France, meanwhile, ninety-eight per
cent of the nation, went on doing, outwardly at least,
very much as it had been doing for generations. Its
men and women had little time to read. They worked
in the fields or in small shops; they paid taxes, tried to
save money and struggled to exist from day to day.

CHAPTER II

The Popular Genres:
Novels, comic and sinister and the Melodrama

↠ *"ALL WOMEN OF FRANCE READ NOVELS," SAID STENDHAL,*
"Often four or five volumes per month, and some as
many as fifteen or twenty."[1]   But all of them did not
have the same degree of education.   For educated
women (to Stendhal, this meant Parisians) there was
the respectable octavo novel which could meet their
severe literary standards.   And for provincials and
chambermaids there was always the popular duodecimo
novel to be rented from lending libraries of provincial
towns.   So great was the gap that popular authors whose
names were on everyone's lips in Marseilles, Bayonne,
Agen or Toulouse were unknown in Paris.

Educated men and women condemned the popular
novel to literary Coventry.   Because of this, and because
it was to loom large, indeed, even threateningly, later in
the century, a careful glance at the origins of the popular
literature becomes a necessity.   Stendhal was right, of
course, but not inclusive enough in his distinction.
Cheap adventure stories were read by chambermaids,

but they were read by men as well as women, humble tradespeople, all who found themselves barred by the boundary lines of the bourgeoisie. Their enthusiasm helped its growth.

Toward the Comic Novel

As it grew, the popular novel quickly developed two main branches: the comic and the sinister or "black" novel. Of the two the comic had the longer ancestry in France. It immediately proclaimed its kinship with the medieval fables and with Rabelais, that Renaissance scholar and joyous vulgarian who did not hesitate to bring chamber pots into his wild stories. It treated lower-class people in good-natured, direct fashion, and, like Rabelais' uninhibited tales, did not boggle at vulgarity. The duodecimo novel continued this old tradition, although its reappearance at this time was somewhat surprising.

Under the ancien régime, well-bred literature had been too polite to pay much attention to the common people or their way of life. True, the seventeenth and eighteenth centuries had occasionally mentioned them but just for the sake of art and always in talking to an elite. Molière had used the peasant and the bourgeois in his plays, but, bourgeois himself, he spoke, hat in hand, to the elegant nobles of Louis XIV's court and was paid to be amusing. Later, Beaumarchais and Diderot used the people to support their literary treatment of eighteenth-century questions, but again, they spoke to a distinguished, sophisticated audience. If they did notice the people, they pretended to ignore them, just as the lush, perfumed beauties of the court pointedly ignored the objects and odors which made the sidewalks of Paris such unpleasant places to cross.

Only late in the eighteenth-century, with Restif de la Bretonne, can one speak of a writer of realistic strain who was himself *peuple* and who wrote about the people accurately. Nicolas-Anne-Aimé Restif de la Bretonne was one of thirteen children of a prosperous peasant family of Yonne. Apprenticed at seventeen as a typesetter, he came (or fled) after two disastrous marriages to Paris where he became a friend of Beaumarchais and gained entry into certain of the capital's salons. Direct knowledge of several levels of French society helped Restif win great popularity with his 42-volume *Les Contemporaines* (1780-85) which he composed directly, without writing, in the printshop itself. His two hundred seventy-two novelettes and four hundred forty-four short stories covered nearly every class of French society, every aspect of Parisian and provincial life. What is more, they treated the people accurately and unblinkingly. For the first time, the butcher, baker and candlestick maker's wife all found a place in literature. Respected writers despised this improbable but highly successful novelist. Benjamin Constant decried the century that could stoop so low as to admire such an author. Hugo took time to sneer at Restif, "who dug the most unhealthy passages in the underground of the masses."[2] Along with complete amorality, a penchant for sensuality and a marked taste for dirty scenes, Restif possessed an unquenchable curiosity which, joined with an acute sense of observation, produced a gift for narration that at times approached genius.

Still, Restif was writing for the upper classes. His

audience was the worldly wealthy of Paris. He amused
and shocked them with his accurate depiction of the
anthill beneath them. He showed them life as the people
lived it just before 1786. However, with the upheavals
and veerings of the Revolution, the public ceased to be
amused by the fantastical extravagances of this strange
man. Understandably, it had other matters on its mind.
So Restif, always needy and always the realist, became a
member of Napoleon's police force, to die, old and forgotten, in 1806.

The honor of winning success by being first both
to write about the people and to write for them fell to
another. Strangely, it fell to an aristocrat, Pigault-
Lebrun. Although not a man of the people, he became
their self-appointed buffoon, writing with the irreligious
wit and emotional responses of what he was, a disabused
ancien régime nobleman. His work showed that he had
understood the lessons of his age. He had quickly
grasped that old times had passed irrevocably, that the
compass north would no longer be foreign policy or
monarchy but, rather, democratization.

His stories showed this clearly. Published from
1822 to 1824, the twenty volumes of novels hardly
differed one from another. Somehow the hero was
always a son of the people who drank like a Swiss,
swore like a sailor but was, withal, a fine fellow. At the
end of each tale the sturdy commoner made his fortune
and married the daughter of a great lord to hearty shouts
of Hurrah for Equality. But before relegating these
novels to a dusty shelf, one should consider again the
audience whom Pigault was addressing. His stories were
aimed straight at readers who still had trouble reading,

who still had to spell out a word from time to time. In short, his audience was the working classes, the people who, from time beyond recollection, had paid feudal taxes, salt taxes, and recently had filled the ranks of Napoleon's armies. Never mind if his novels were poor things. For once here was a writer not only talking about the people but talking straight to the very ones he was describing. He was telling them precisely what they wanted to hear: amusing stories based squarely upon lower-class realities.

Comedy has always used reality as its base; Pigault's stories treated the anguishes of footmen, coachmen and other lesser literary fry. His fiction was popular because it mixed an easy tear or so with the beginnings of a wicked smile. His audience, like audiences of all times, laughed at the pratfalls of others and sneaked admiring glances at a woman's generous charms. Like their better-mannered brethren, his readers wanted to believe in a happy ending, so he provided it. The populace found Pigault's sentimentality and earthy comedies exactly to their taste. They bought his work and read it tirelessly.

So Pigault-Lebrun created the comic novel of the Restoration by writing both to the people and about them. His huge popularity also created an even larger audience for the popular novel. Not surprisingly, numerous men followed him in treating the comic ups and downs of life among tradespeople and petty employees. One of his best known followers was Paul de Kock.

Employed at fifteen as a petty Parisian bank clerk, de Kock was fired when it was discovered that he had written a novel with the disquieting title *My Wife's Baby*. The book was not a success, but with his second attempt, *Georgette, or the Scrivener's Daughter* (1820), he began a long succession of best-selling novels that brought him worldwide fame. His works total some 299 volumes. Even for a man with remarkable facility, who could write a play in twenty-four hours and a novel in two weeks, the total is still staggering. Ordinary mortals are reassured, if a bit disappointed, when they learn that de Kock's novels are really just the same novel, written and rewritten, repeated endlessly with only small changes of décor and accessories.

One of his many variations on the same theme is his *Concierge of the Rue du Bac*. In it we find a geometrical crisscrossing of domestic life and love. The story concerns two men, both servants in the same rich household. Droguin, an arrogant doorman, scorns Robertin (the concierge of the title) and loves devotedly his own flighty daughter Iphigenia. Unfortunately Iphigenia strays into the dangerous ways of the upper classes and ends by becoming the mistress of a young nobleman, thus betraying her father's trust. Robertin's son, Julian, an honest and unassuming young worker, timidly worships Droguin's other daughter, Adeline. As an obvious punishment for Droguin's arrogance his daughter Iphigenia comes to a bad end, while Julian marries his beloved Adeline.

Today's reader may well wonder what possible interest the public of that time could have found in so many replayings of this same plot. It must have been clear to even the least sophisticated reader that the thread of his story was exceedingly thin. Where was the interest? Part of the answer lay in de Kock's choosing his characters from the common people. This substratum of society was totally familiar to the people but yet new to the reader. Grocers, delivery boys, doormen and indigent music teachers constituted a surprising *dramatis personae.* Nor should it be forgotten that in this undistinguished world adventures rained like hail stones but no real blood was shed. The suitor hurrying to meet his beloved was not stabbed, tortured or shot; instead he received . . . a chamber pot upon his head, or a nasty rip in the seat of his trousers from an angry dog. Dowagers of pouter-pigeon proportions were suddenly enmeshed in unwished-for, ludicrous intimacy with indignant, balding financiers. A sample of such goings on may help characterize the particular mixture that de Kock specialized in. One of his heroes, Gustave, speaks of a scrape he has barely managed to get out of.

> With just a little bit of foresight I wouldn't have gone to that wedding . . . Mrs. Ratel wouldn't have told me that she wets her bed when she drinks water, the young widow wouldn't have come down into the garden with me . . . that stupid cabinet maker wouldn't have fought with me; I wouldn't have a black eye and a swollen nose, the groom wouldn't have gone off to look for his hat in the little closet where his "better half" was hiding with that other poor fool who would have had plenty of time to take her garters on and off three or four times, and poor Lolotte wouldn't have stuck her rear end in the well because the fire wouldn't have burned her dress . . .[3]

Accompanying the constant humor, the unending Gallic gaiety, was the warming assurance that essentially such reading was both pleasurable and moral! Even bourgeois readers enjoyed de Kock. A hero might be permitted an occasional adulterous frolic—boys will be boys—so long as the reader knew that he would inevitably settle into an irreproachably moral relationship with a heroine sweet and pure. From first to last, one was certain that, although de Kock might take certain momentary liberties with the dignified Dame of Bourgeois Morality, he would write nothing really shocking. Didn't he always conclude in favor of husband, not lover; of virtue, not vice? Closely examined, the novels showed that true morality was always safeguarded.

When critics deplored his lack of style, de Kock answered by affirming that he was making his characters speak as the people actually spoke. But it really did not matter very much. The people bought his novels because they liked seeing their own lives and circumstances reflected in them.

The Sinister Novel

French hack writers, pricked by the success of the English Gothic romance, quickly pirated its techniques and produced the sinister novel. Of these writers, Ducray-Duminil, a journeyman novelist, was the speediest in using the new English devices. In 1796 he published a four-volume story, *Victor or the Child of the Forest,* and two years later another popular novel in five volumes, *Coelina or the Child of Mystery.* Both stories, duodecimo, showed an unmistakable strain of English Gothic. There was the unfortunate young girl of mysterious birth ready to suffer; her faithful fiancé willing to risk all to enjoy the sweet fruits of his fidelity; a scoundrel sufficiently evil to function in terrifying fashion, and finally the servants, garrulous and credulous, to provide moments of comic relief. Just like Mrs. Radcliffe's, Ducray-Duminil's novels used mysterious noises, groans, piteous characters, subterranean caverns, imprisoned ghostlike figures and apparently supernatural happenings.   Further, just as Ann Radcliffe had done, Ducray-Duminil took time at the very end to explain away these mysteries. What was more, the action, mood and baleful style were astonishingly similar to hers. Even today *Coelina* gives off a musty emanation:

> A strange noise strikes her frightened senses:
> the noise seems that of a horn giving off a
> long and dragging sound. She listens, the noise
> stops .   .   . she listens again: this sound,
> lengthy and painful, is prolonged and strikes
> again her now attentive ears . . . these
> lugubrious sounds . . . resemble exactly but
> even louder, the painful gasps of a dying man
> who is ready to depart this life.[4]

Quite evidently the new foreign additive did give increased literary mileage: *Coelina* was reprinted at least eleven times between 1798 and 1825.   It is not at all surprising then to find that Ducray-Duminil's third novel, *Paul, or the Abandoned Farm* (1800), employed a setting still more Gothic: an old castle half in ruins, long corridors along which sounded mysterious footsteps, underground rooms into which one dared not enter, ghosts moving about with torches in their hands. With *Victor, Coelina* and *Paul*, the popular novel of terror, the sinister novel, was launched. Ducray-Duminil was not alone in adopting English terror techniques. Many other hack writers saw the advantages of this new literary device and hastened to use it. It proved long lived as well as popular: some twenty years later Balzac paid Ducray-Duminil the compliment of imitating him. Such was its durability that the popular fiction—the comic and the sinister—remained best sellers throughout the early Restoration.

While the oligarchy was pursuing its monarchical and literary chase into the royalist past, and while the elite read Scott, the people rented from lending libraries novels by their own favorite authors. Even as late as 1832, in the small town of Narbonne, the best-selling, or best-renting, authors were men the elite had never heard of: Jouy d'Arlincourt, Victor Ducange, Pigault-Lebrun, Ducray-Duminil and Paul de Kock. These writers of popular sinister novels provided the raw material for the other important literary genre of the people, the melodrama.

The Melodrama

This dramatic hybrid made its appearance in France at just about the same time as the popular novel. It too had its origins in the people and evolved under odd and interesting circumstances.

For centuries, Paris, like many French towns, had celebrated the coming of spring or the autumn harvest season with elaborate fairs. These celebrations, which cannot have been too different from the traditional

American country fairs, had all the competitions one might expect for breeders of animals, bakers of pies, sewers of fine seams and masters in all the arts of husbandry and domesticity. In addition the fairs had the tradition-hallowed sideshows of magicians, strongmen, jugglers, tightrope walkers, curiously deformed animals, shadow plays and marionettes. Over the years these performers had established their right to operate small booths where they attempted to attract their own audiences and to extract what money they could from them.

The melodrama had its origins in the booths housing the marionette shows. Here, where music and dancing were the main entertainments, where coarse joking provided the humor, marionette spectacles and tableaux were offered to the simpler folk of Paris. Since competition for their hard-earned sous was fierce, music was added to the puppet pantomimes, martial, patriotic or pathetic, as needed to heighten the effect of the tableaux. Then one of the booth owners substituted live actors for his puppets. Others followed his example and took the next step of having the actors speak while acting out the crude dramas that developed from the former unmoving tableaux, while music continued to sharpen the emotion of the moment. Even untrained and untutored as these entertainers were, the offerings of their booths soon encroached upon the field of the jealous legitimate theaters. One booth owner was haled into court and legally enjoined to limit his offerings to tightrope walkers and pantomimes. But little by little the legitimate theaters were obliged to abandon their efforts at self protection. The booths continued to offer

The elegant theater of the cultivated Parisians, the Théâtre Français.

The Theater Porte St. Martin, a popular melodrama house.

more and more lavishly staged, lengthier dramas, with music adding to the attraction of the spectacle. From simple puppet shows the booth owners had progressed to a kind of public dramatic offering embellished with music and dancing that became known as music-plays (melo-dramas).

So popular were these crude dramas that the performances continued even after the fair season had ended. In Paris, booth owners moved to a street with four rows of shade trees and a pleasant walk which had become the popular promenade for lower-class Parisians. Little by little the booths grew into full-fledged theaters, and the street became known as the Boulevard du Crime, after the criminal misdeeds in which the melodramas soon specialized. These recently arrived theaters were centered in the poorer quarter of Saint Martin where their audiences lived. Since there were no government subsidies they depended quite directly upon pleasing their patrons.

What was the general composition of the audiences? In general, it consisted of small shopkeepers, workers and domestics. As Stendhal explained it, Parisians had a marked taste for the theater. But whereas in London both high and low classes attended the same performance, viewing it from either box seat or from the pit, "In Paris, we have theaters exclusively reserved for the lower classes." He went on to explain that "half of the French peasants had acquired some land, respectability and a certain degree of education. In those days it was the artisans of Paris, a group recruited from the peasants of all France, that frequented the theaters of the Boulevard."[5]

Their taste in drama was quite unlike that of their upper-class cousins. The people wanted violent emotions, strong contrasts, tears and laughter juxtaposed, never mind how clumsily, and an unvarying adherence to a morality which required that virtue be rewarded and vice punished. The action had to be gripping, surprising in its incidents and overwhelming in its effect. In these theaters the playwright was faced with an audience that had come to know exactly what it wanted, was paying for and fully intended to get. The playwrights obeyed the mandate of their public; they pared down the graceful but time-consuming transitions, gratingly juxtaposed bathos and coarse humor and succeeded in giving their audience a resounding emotional thump.

Out of the interplay between the offerings of the theaters and the approval of the patrons came a certain body of subject matter, variations upon successful themes and proven ways of presenting them which established the new theater in the affection of the public and in a quite predictable pattern. And since later changes came from this beginning, a glance at the melodrama in its first form is required.

There were four essential roles in each melodrama. First, a tyrant or villain whose soul, animated by the most wicked of passions, was soiled with every sort of sin. The villain occupied himself with lengthy victimizing of the second of the four characters, the unfortunate heroine, and the poor actress obliged to create this role served as a vehicle for suffering virtue. For the third part the hero was an absolute necessity. If virtue be its own reward in real life, in the melodrama it invariably stood in desperate need of protection. Finally, there was the *niais,* or ninny, to provide laughter when the audience had had enough of snuffling. The villain persecuted the unfortunate heroine until the gamut of misfortune had been run, at which time the Protector of Innocence arrived and, with the help of the ninny, righted all wrongs and punished the villain.

All of this was divided into three acts. The first was devoted to love, the second to misfortune and the third to the triumph of love and the punishment of evil. Throughout the three acts, speech was couched in an imposingly sententious prose notable for the frequency of moral maxims and the heavy overuse of epithets. The "bells of evening" paralleled the "voice of nature." The "vile seducer" lusted endlessly after an impeccably "virtuous woman" despite the remonstrances of a "venerable old man." Music was liberally used to accompany stage entries and departures and to underline dramatic situations. All in all, these melodramas were crude things and all too pragmatically put together.

But despite the obvious weaknesses of the genre, or rather, because of them—the plays did, after all, deliver a tremendous emotional punch—the melodrama achieved an incredible success. First popularized and stoutly supported by the lower classes, the genre soon attracted the attention and popularity of the upper classes. The Boulevard theaters even became quite fashionable. Weeping was no longer restricted to redfaced concierges and shopgirls; refined young misses shed just as many tears. Sobbings into kerchiefs were democratically shared at performances of "The Little Peasheller" or "Love's Labyrinth." Simple, direct and clumsy, their attraction was more than enough to frighten the legitimate stages where

PHYSIONOMIES THÉATRALES (*Boulevard du Temple.*)
(D'après la lithographie de Pruche.)

better-trained if much less popular actors declaimed their cadenced alexandrines. These cultivated tragedies provided little competition for the melodrama.

The difficulty for the popular drama was in finding enough material to answer its audiences' demands for something new, always something new. Writers of melodramas turned to the novels and stories of the day. Since the English Gothic novel was enjoying a huge vogue, they turned it rapidly, if not always too neatly, into melodrama. Scott alone was a large vein of rich ore that the French were not slow to mine. His enormous popularity almost guaranteed success to any stage adaptation. Shakespeare too was put to brisk use by these clumsy literary alchemists. The drama critic for *Le Constitutionnel* complained that "the theater is going to serve us up Shakespeare wholesale and retail . . ."[6]

Then, having stripmined as much from the English as they easily could, the writers for this insatiable audience turned avidly to the popular novels and stories of their own nation. One writer noted that Ducray-Duminil's recent novels, *Victor* and *Coelina,* were very popular among just the same lower-class audience that attended the melodrama. What more natural than to make *Victor* into a drama? As luck would have it, *Victor* was a smash hit running for 392 performances at the Ambigu-Comique theater. The adaptor, René-Charles-Guilbert de Pixérécourt, was beginning his career as father of the melodrama. Encouraged by *Victor*'s success, Pixérécourt, an erstwhile painter of ladies' fans, turned once more to Ducray-Duminil adapting *Coelina* for the stage and finding success at the same theater. But this time he had really done it. In Paris, *Coelina* had a run of 387 performances and in the provinces an additional run of some 1,429. Pixérécourt had arrived, and with him the melodrama in its first full flowering. For the next thirty years his fertile pen provided entertainment that delighted the public. It also tempted into imitation other men who should have known better: Balzac, Dumas, even the towering Hugo. For readers of today a closer look at Pixérécourt's *Coelina* is vital, for the play—as complicated as it is—furnishes a perfectly typical example of his product.

Monsieur Dufour, the honorable guardian of his niece, Coelina, as well as of her inherited fortune, hesitates out of honest scruples to marry her to his own son, Stephany, even though the two young people are in love. Then a certain Monsieur Truguelin, his son and a rascally servant appear at Dufour's home. Truguelin is shaken to see there a guest of the household, a man named Francisque Humbert, and, mysteriously enough, Humbert himself trembles upon seeing Truguelin but is unable to say a word. The audience learns that Humbert had earlier been the victim of two men who had attacked him and left him for dead. Humbert had recovered but had lost his "organs of speech." In reality, the elder Truguelin and his insidious servant are the very men who had attacked Humbert and who now plot to kill him. Then Truguelin suddenly produces a document which shows that Coelina is really not Dufour's niece nor is she entitled to the large inheritance that Dufour had so honorably preserved for her; she is actually the fruit of an illegitimate union between Truguelin's daughter and Humbert. Humbert recognizes his own daughter in Coelina, and in unspeakable sadness he and Coelina depart Dufour's household to trudge the inhospitable countryside. Truguelin is finally unmasked and forced to take to his heels, philosophizing as he leaves that "if one only knew what it cost to leave the path of virtue, there would be very few doers of misdeeds upon the earth."[7]

A decent concern for the reader's peace of mind obliges us to add that after two hairpin bends in the road of this dramatic juggernaut, the curse of bastardy is removed from Coelina who is then free to marry Stephany. Truguelin has seen the error of his ways, and the honorable Dufour extends his arms to the mute Humbert, exclaiming, "I hold you again in my esteem!"[8]

Audiences of that day shivered and wept. Today's audience finds itself divided between embarrassment and amusement. But, dated as the play sounds to our ears and bad as it doubtless was, its popularity in Parisian and provincial theaters attested to its emotional appeal. What, then, could have been the charm of this new sort of theatrical offering? One does not, after all, reconstruct the history of a period by merely making fun of it.

The answer lies in this: the public of that time was accustomed to spectacles in which machinery, changes of scene and costume were the attractions. Suddenly it was thrilled by a play in which human emotions were given full rein. This change, strongly stated in *Coelina,* was a revelation. The dialogue, badly written first by Ducray-Duminil and made still worse by Pixérécourt, was nonetheless a rendering of the passions and sentiments of people who were believable. The action, almost contemporary, took place in a modest milieu, and was the result of an attempt to depict real human beings in real situations. After all, bastards were and still are a problem for people in society, inheritances do bring about squabbles and greed does motivate people. No matter how summary the characterization and how stereotyped the people, this drama represented a distinct move away from artificiality toward reality. One need not smile too broadly at seeing Ducray-Duminil review the play taken from his novel. He termed it "warm, tightly written and, especially, natural . . . the best work that has been played on the boulevard and worthy of the finest theaters."[9]

The public seemed to agree with him. The hundred or so similar plays that followed *Coelina* prove that Pixérécourt's popularity was not a momentary fluke. Another of his plays, *The Wife with Two Husbands,* had a Paris run of 451 performances and almost an additional thousand in the provinces. One line will serve to characterize this masterwork: "An offended father who pardons is the most perfect earthly image of God."[10] And audiences loved it.

But not even he wrote only successes. Some failed or had short runs. One such, *Christopher Columbus,* attempted a realistic representation of the discovery of America. But spectators were doubless mystified to hear conversation among natives in what was averred to be the language of the Antilles. For an entire scene savages conversed on stage in the following tongue:

Oranko: Cati louma.
Karaka: Amouliaca Azakia Kerebek (Oranko
hesitates) [!]

Oranko: Inalaki Chicalamai . . .
Karaka: Arexhoui azakia, avaiti-avou[11]

Understandably this play ran for only 117 performances. The toll of popularity upon creativity began to
tell: Pixérécourt was tiring.   Other writers of such
dramas were needed. As always, some came forward.
A few even found success. Louis Charles Caigniez (1762-
1842) enriched several theaters although he was never
able to find wealth for himself.   His *Judgment of
Solomon* earned some 300,000 francs for the theater
but only 900 for him.

Caigniez's play showed the characters and events
which led, after certain meanderings, to Solomon's judgment in the last moments of the drama. First one sees a
lovely Jewess, Leila, beloved of a prince incognito.
Abandoned by him, she keeps his child which is stolen
one day. Later she learns that her prince is to be married
to the noble widow, Tamira, thought to be barren but
to whom a child had unexpectedly been born.   The
audience, along with Leila, sees through the transparent
substitution of Leila's child for that of the matron.
Moved to protest, Leila asks justice. Both women find
themselves in the august presence of the king, and the
expected scene takes place. The true mother is identi-
fied, the prince reappears, recognizes virtue and claims
Leila as his one and only love. The haughty matron,
Tamira, suddenly finds herself "enlightened by a supernatural power" and accepts the decision as just. Maidens,
of whom there seems to have been a large supply, have
been mustering onstage during the last moments. They
now come together, approach the audience and sing

while the curtain falls:

Leila sees on this great day her cruel pains
end.
Let us wish her happiness, let us pardon love's
error.
Let us see in her only the model of maternal
tenderness.[12]

All ended happily and the audience was content to have seen justice triumph, one must suppose. But at least one of Caigniez's plays had enough merit to be translated into English (*The Magpie Thief, or the Servant of Palaisseau*), and after pleasing audiences at Drury Lane it served as the libretto for Rossini's opera *La Gazza Ladra*.

As the decade of 1810-1820 came to a close, Pixérécourt and Caigniez were played less and less. The careers of the two men whom the public had been pleased to name the Corneille and Racine of the Boulevards very nearly paralleled one another. Both had come to popularity on the Boulevard du Crime after the turn of the century, and both were realizing a sharp decline in popularity when another younger man came to take his own place as the third of the kings of the melodrama, in 1820.

Victor Ducange (1783-1833) turned to writing when the Restoration deprived him of his modest governmental position. From 1820 until his death in 1833, it was he who dominated the boulevard theaters: his *Theresa or the Orphan of Geneva* was staged in 1820, *The Sorceress* (from Scott's *Guy Mannering*) in 1821,

Lisbeth, adapted from one of his own novels, in 1823. In 1827 Ducange's best-known work and probably one of the most applauded of all melodramas, *Thirty Years or the Life of a Gambler,* moved and horrified its audiences. It impressed even the well-bred *Globe* which called it a "great tragedy . . . a most complete and vigorous drama."[13]

In the first act of this breathless drama the audience sees Georges de Germany receive his father's curse in a shattering scene. Then step by step, Georges descends the cellar stairs of infamy. Driven by his fatal passion for gambling, he commits, in ascending order, almost every sort of sin. Georges' clothing changes from stylish to old clothes and finally to rags. Accompanying him is the most patient of loving and forebearing wives known to literature. In the third act Georges is driven to "take up the knife of the assassin." He plots to rob and kill a travelling stranger who, as sound staging will have it, is none other than his own son returning home with a large sum of money to help his parents in their distress. Georges hides and plans to assassinate the traveller, whose identity remains unknown to all but the audience. Georges crouches, knife at the ready; he strikes. The young man staggers back, wounded but not mortally; assassin and assailed recognize one another. The father, overcome by the enormity of his crime, and realizing the degradation which inevitably results from dice and cards, has just enough true manliness left in him for one last act of expiation. In a frenzy of guilt he scuttles into the flaming cabin he had thought to use to destroy the body of his victim, and so brings his own life to a horrid end.

Tears flowed as seldom before in a theater. Women sobbed for the patient, virtuous and pitiful wife. It was too much for the most hardened critics to bear. Even the usually caustic Jules Janin melted into praise, declaring that Victor Ducange had given his drama "an important and great moral utility."[14]

And Ducange kept it up, writing one melodrama after another. After the Revolution of 1830 and the removal of Charles X's stern censorship, he collaborated with an aging Pixérécourt to produce *The Jesuit* (taken from one of Ducange's novels) and *The Three Daughters of the Widow*. When Ducange died in 1833, Janin marked his passing by a surprisingly gentle obituary in the *Journal des Débats*:

> The death of Victor Ducange leaves the Boulevards prey to that crowd of young people . . . who spend their time composing gravely great dramas . . . Victor Ducange needs no funeral oration; his replacements will make us miss him quite enough.[15]

One detects in the clipped words of Janin a certain nostalgia for the passing not just of Ducange but of the melodrama in its first youthful exuberance. Thirteen years later Théophile Gautier, that impeccable poet and former romantic, celebrated the bombast and headlong rush of early melodrama.

> O Guilbert de Pixérécourt, O Caigniez, O Victor Ducange . . . language has changed greatly since these great masters.[16]

Indeed it had, but not only language. With the sudden shift in rulers in 1830 the melodrama was able to increase its scope. Without the snappish censors of Charles X to fear, it could be more topical, treat contemporary politics and immediate social concerns. As it began to do just this, the worthy bourgeois became perplexed; they did not know what to make of it. Increasingly, the new popular theater chose its heroes from the populace and drew its villains from the better people, respectable people. Bankers and property-owners as villains? They grew uneasy and concluded, without understanding it, that plays which attacked their social class and its treasured possessions were simply immoral. Pixérécourt himself, ingenuous and baffled, spoke out of an obvious hurt in complaining that "today's authors don't do as I did." Why, he asked, don't their plays resemble mine? And then he came to his own answer which reassured him; it was because they lacked his heart, his sensitivity, and his conscience.

To understand the melodrama, which after 1830 became progressively more socially concerned, it is necessary to examine the psychology and stereotypes of its pre-1830 existence. Obliged to reflect the morality of its audience and obliged also to remain a "drama in a hurry," this early theater had not time to do much more than sketch stock characters who approached the ultimate in abstraction: the hero, heroine and villain. They were shown with little of the complexity of verisimilitude as our time perceives it. On this stage, all fathers were kind but stern, white-haired and dignified. Daughters invariably loved them and preferred their company to that of young men. Of course these young maidens

SPECTACLE GRATIS A L'AMBIGU-COMIQUE

(D'après le tableau de Boilly, 1819.)

A LA PORTE SAINT-MARTIN
d'après le dessin de Damourette.

were pure, they never acted pettishly, fussed or slammed doors. Heroes were veritable Galahads in the purity of their intentions, brave, courageous. They were as extreme in their way as the villains who were condemned to a monotonous series of joyless evil-doings that were always terminated by last minute foilings. On this stage, good had to triumph. Moreover, the world these characters lived in was a sort of Benjamin Franklin one in which merit and money were almost synonymous. Wealth, even modest, was almost unvaryingly the reward of hard work, economy and personal merit. People, posited good or bad at the play's opening, were rewarded or punished at the end of the third act. The morality of the popular stage required this. Such, then, was the melodrama as its first period drew to an end. What had begun at the turn of the century with Pixérécourt finally closed its curtains three decades later with the death of Victor Ducange.

CHAPTER III

Politics and the Popular Novel

➤➤   *STENDHAL ASSERTED THAT BRINGING POLITICS INTO THE*
novel was like firing a pistol shot in a cathedral. The
comparison of the cultivated literature with the remote
sanctity of a church was most apt. The wan, delicately-
fashioned Restoration novel of manners had held itself
aloof from the hurly-burly of actual life. But popular
literature could easily include the explosive issue of
politics. Alive and much more immediately responsive
to day-to-day excitements, it had no qualms about including one more bit of contemporaneity. If writers for
the people seldom went further than quick raillery about
such matters, it was because Restoration censorship was
severe. Nonetheless, there was one highly successful
popular novelist who openly brought politics into his
writings. Interestingly, Stendhal knew of him and re-
viewed his novels with praise.

Victor Ducange reacted sharply, even passionately,
to the political and social issues of his times. He was
among the first popular writers to voice any consistent

and serious social criticism in his writings. Out of conviction Ducange sympathized with and championed the people of France. As clearly as Stendhal he saw a nation divided into two bitterly opposed camps: the powerful, the rich, the noble and the rest of France trying to take wobbly beginners' steps toward democracy. His fiction reflected his liberal political position and his unyielding opposition to the Restoration Monarchy. Written from 1819 to 1833, Ducange's novels appraised sharply the reigns of three monarchs, Louis XVIII, Charles X and Louis Philippe. Stendhal wrote that he was one of the very few novelists who painted France as it really was in stories that contained a great deal of truth although very little art.[1]

Because he was the first to take the popular novel into the terrain of social criticism at a time when censors were strict and punishment sharp, and because he was able to do this and still find best-selling popularity, Ducange's stories deserve careful attention. A study of their themes, settings and characters is revelatory and rewarding.

Ducange practised both the comic and the sinister novel and frequently mixed the two together. From our knowledge of the sinister genre we may quite reasonably expect to find in his stories, just as in his melodramas, certain stock characters: a hero, a heroine and a villain (or villainess). We may also confidently expect that hero and villain will represent, as in the crudest of morality plays, the "good" and "bad," the north and south poles of behavior.

Of his first three novels, *Agatha* (1819), *Albert* (1820) and *Valentine* (1921), only the latter two are interesting. *Agatha* was nothing more than a light comic love story much like those of Pigault-Lebrun or Paul de Kock. But *Albert or The Missionary Lovers* had an emphatically contemporary story to tell of Congregation missionaries and Jesuits. The tale was a mixture of the comic novel with its springtime and roses love story and the sinister with its villains and fearful conspiracies.

Albert, a young ex-officer of Napoleon's armies, was of humble birth but loved Amelia, the daughter of an ambitious petty noble family. To forestall Amelia's forced marriage to an old but wealthy man, the young pair ran away and joined a band of rascals who travelled from town to town masquerading as Jesuit missionaries. Unnumbered episodes later, the young couple were helped by the mock priests in arranging a true marriage ceremony so that love might triumph legitimately. In his title, Ducange made timely use—and in his story made belly laughter mockery—of an organization that was, in reality, no laughing matter. In fact, for its opponents and for its advocates, the Congregation was a deadly serious affair.

This Catholic organization had begun with the seemingly innocuous object of developing the field of good works and of defending the faith against evil examples. As it grew rapidly in size and influence under the restored monarchy, it attracted the deepest suspicions of political liberals and the lively animosity of all but the most fervid altar-and-throne catholics. Even in the Chamber, many exclaimed loudly that the nation was in the grips of a huge conspiracy. In the eyes of all anticlerical Frenchmen, the Congregation became synonymous with secret and subversive plotting.

Nor were such suspicions entirely ill founded. In truth, the Congregation had established branches in all principal French cities, had drawn members from the upper bourgeoisie and the highest officials of the French church. It had indeed become an instrument of the ultra-royalists. Moreover, there was a faction of the group, a truly secret society, controlled by the extreme conservatives whose clandestine efforts were aimed at influencing the Chamber, the press, the governmental brueaucracy and even the courts. Understandably, the Congregation was controversial. But even more disquieting, and arousing still more resentment among the people, was an arm of the order that was quite openly visible. This was the missionary branch called the Missions of France which sought to win back the many sheep lost to the church while France had been without its king and its clergy.

To achieve this goal, well organized and well supported missions of the Congregation were sent out into the provinces to preach and exhort. Typically, a group of four or five missionaries drawn from the swollen ranks of the unemployed clergy took themselves to a provincial town where they preached fervently for several weeks preparing their listeners for a final high solemn ceremony of reparation. In this, a huge cross weighing sometimes as much as a thousand kilos was carried by sweating teams of the faithful in relays to the spot where it was to be placed. As the procession wended its way through the town, behind the cross marched all the authorities of the locality: the bishop, the prefect of police, the military commander, and behind them all those who thought it wise or prudent to make a public showing of piety. At the site and beneath the approving glances of the powerful, the people made public reparation to the cross for the outrages it had received since the Revolution: reparation for offenses committed towards neighbors, reparation for the injury done to Louis XVI, to Marie Antoinette and to the family of the King. Sometimes a bonfire was held, a bookburning fueled by the impious works of Voltaire and Jean-Jacques Rousseau of which the returned faithful had purged their libraries. The audience shouted acclaim to the words of the priests. While the crowds did public penance, the missionaries distributed chapelets, medallions, scapularies and images. These were received to the chant of canticles sung by choirs of young men and women. The ceremony ended with a sermon in which the people were exhorted to maintain religion and legitimate government; i.e., Monarchy.

In *Albert*, Jesuits and missionaries were Ducange's targets and he struck at them tirelessly. His fictional revivalists alternated between broad burlesque and horrid villainy. In parody of actual ceremonies, the mock Jesuits set to work in a small provincial town. One member of the group arranged for the sale of catechisms, canticles and letters certified to have fallen straight from heaven. Another sold relics and amulets from a counter he set up in the foyer of the church while a third member was charged with the details of the great sermon, the public penance and the planting of the cross. When Amelia, bewildered by all of this, asked why the band of criminals was masquerading as Jesuits, the leader of the group explained. "People call out to us, they open their arms to us . . . the faithful bring us chickens and truffles; little girls confess and open their hearts to us; money pours into our pockets."[2]   In this novel, rascals disguised as Jesuits provided easy comedy; the true villains were the real Jesuits.

Another quite genuine social concern treated by Ducange was education, a matter about which both the people and the ruling oligarchy were deeply concerned. In actual fact, education in Restoration France was in desperate straits.   There were not enough schools or properly trained teachers, not enough money to build the one or to train the other.   To make matters worse, the entire question had become political.   Royalists and Liberals differed bitterly in Chamber debates while the people waited, apprehensive and resentful.

The Royalists favored education in church-supported and maintained schools.   The Liberals were loud in demanding a public system of education.   Anticlerical as they were, the Liberals held it a matter of principle that there exist in any village of France a school and a schoolmaster who were not the natural allies of the distrusted Church.   But the quarrel went further; the clergy favored a teaching method rather like the one practiced in America's one-room schoolhouses.   In this, all children of all grades met together while the teacher taught the different subjects and different levels as best he could.   The system was difficult but workable; besides it had the great advantage, as the conservatives saw it, of preserving the principle of authority.   The Liberals touted the superiority of the mutual instruction system, a kind of each-one-teach-one method which allowed a single teacher to use student instructors.   Many more students could be dealt with in the same amount of time.

Ducange simplified the issue. He burlesqued a conversation between an important townslady and the mayor as to where the church school and the public school buildings should be located. At her prompting, he assigned the public school to an old, wet, dark and dank hovel whose walls were crumbling and situated at the very edge of town and found for the church school just the opposite: a clean healthy spacious building right near the church. Readers of that day understood.

But not content with melodramatic picturing of villainy or with broad satire, Ducange burst out again and again in direct and impassioned speech to his readers and to the powerful men of the government.

> You who govern men, how much trouble you
> take to be hated! And how easy it would be
> for you to be adored . . . [you] treat these
> men who pay for your palaces, your armies
> and your ministers like vile sheep.[3]

Despite its tender love scenes, its bashful kisses and its blond Amelia to engage readers, *Albert* was a searing denunciation of the Congregation and the missionaries of the early eighteen-twenties.

The third of Ducange's novels, *Valentine or the Pastor of Uzès,* took place during the White Terror following the hundred days of Napoleon's return to France from St. Helena. This terror took its name from the white of the Bourbon coat of arms and the revenge which the royalists took upon their enemies, principally those who had wavered in their loyalty to Louis XVIII and who had even returned to the Emperor's colors.

For weeks during 1815 Royalists and bands of thugs and criminals roved the countryside of southern France methodically robbing and murdering any who were thought to be guilty of the "crime" of the hundred days or even so much as uttering seditious remarks. Some hundred and thirty people were slaughtered. Louis's government was probably not guilty of encouraging the murder but it did little or nothing to stop it. The important thing was to return the people to monarchy.

Ducange used *Valentine* to lash out again and again at the twin enemies of intolerant catholicism and political repression. His audience had not forgotten the horrors of a terror only six years earlier. In portraying the destruction of a humble Protestant family, Ducange was simply reflecting popular fears from the perspective of the people. This was the world as seen from beneath the surface of French Restoration society.

The hero, the son of the title's pastor, was Adrien. He was twenty-one, energetic and, of course, well mannered. Valentine was the heroine, a young foundling brought up by the pastor and, at fourteen, a paragon of youthful virtue and blossoming physical charms. The two fell in love slowly enough to allow the author (and the reader) quite his fill of scenes describing Valentine's flowering and Adrien's impatient chastity. Their marriage ceremony was interrupted by the sudden arrival of an evil countess and a scheming Spanish Jesuit priest who abducted the young bride-to-have-been. Chapters later, Adrien rescued his beloved from the horrors of the Terror, saw his own saintly Protestant father murdered and finally succeeded in gaining the frontier of

Switzerland. There, from safety, he bewailed the fate of a France torn by villainies and injustices.

In *Valentine* Ducange presented his readers with an implacably evil and plotting noblewoman who was always accompanied by the treacherous Jesuit, Father Simeon. Certainly the Jesuits were cordially disliked and even feared in France; their return in 1815 caused a great stir among almost all the French. But in his evil countess Ducange was playing upon a dislike that was truly nation-wide.

The Duchess of Angoulême was seemingly fated to displease the French. She was the daughter of Louis XVI. She had been imprisoned along with her parents at the Revolution, had all but watched their deaths at the guillotine, had scrawled upon her cell wall a little girl's prayer to God to forgive their killers. When finally released to freedom, she had gone only to dreary exile in England. Yet when she returned in the entourage of Louis XVIII in 1815, she was viewed with complete mistrust and dislike, fear and contempt. Disagreeable in appearance and distant in her personality, she was widely thought to exercise great influence upon the King in matters religious. Hers was the hand seen behind every unpopular measure taken in affairs of religion. Upon her fell the blame for all acts of religious vengeance, for the concessions granted to the Jesuits. Fatally, she became in fiction a figure of menace and a target for mockery; writers had only to allude to a noblewoman of great haughtiness and religiosity for the public to recognize the victim of the jibe.

Sometimes the Duchess (or Marquise, or Baronness) was used in the popular novel for nothing more important than a bit of easy comedy. In others she provided melodramatic thrills: the relentless, conspiring, bloodthirsty noblewoman guided and abetted by her wily Jesuit cohort. Ducange's marquise bore a caricatured resemblance to the unfortunate woman. He had his marquise join the Congregation where she met the sophistical Father Simeon. He it was who taught her such trickeries as "mental restriction" and "interior oaths" and, in secret rites, allowed her to see all the beasts of the apocalypse and naked angels in the form of handsome young men.

And then Ducange went too far. In an incident every bit as bloodthirsty as the English Gothic novel could ever have devised, he obliged his marquise to murder a young woman who was in process of giving birth. His language was quite equal to Sade's worst in his description of the horrid affair.

> They dragged the unfortunate woman from the bed where she lay trembling. They put a gag in her mouth; they dragged her by the hair into the fatal room. They beat her cruelly; these horrors were calculated to provoke other pains that she soon experienced. Then they bound her hands, stretched her out upon the floor . . . the dead child, torn to shreds, was devoured by a dreadful animal. The cadaver of the young woman was covered up with the marquise's clothing.[4]

Decidedly this went far beyond the bounds of the permissible in alluding to real people. Most emphatically, one could not invent characters who behaved as his marquise had and allow them to have even the slightest resemblance to the Duchess of Angoulême. The government seized the novel, brought Ducange to trial and sentenced him to six months in prison.

This stay behind bars accomplished part of its goal: it taught Ducange a bit of caution. His next novel, *The Widow's Three Daughters*, was a light love story, as bland and uncontroversial as sugared pabulum. He could not resist, though, adding a preface to it in which he at once protested his total innocence in alluding to the Duchess— why, he did not even know the worthy woman!—and continued his attacks upon the church of Rome and Louis' government. He made sure, however, that this time his remarks were general enough not to get him into trouble. He limited himself to rhetorical demands for a religion one could take seriously, priests whose robes did not stink of infamy. But even as he wrote he warmed to his task. The people, he warned, would no longer be had by deceit, intimidation or repression; they were a bit too experienced now. No more parades! The populace would hoot such things down. They already knew all the stage tricks of throne and altar; they had already seen too much of actors and stage make-up. The masses might well continue to be the victims of the royalist government but they would certainly not be its dupes.

Ducange wrote now with the earned bitterness of his six months imprisonment. More, he was writing what the lower classes themselves felt, deeply and with finality. French royalists wanted to turn back the hands of the clock, to reestablish the ancien régime, to set in place the paraphernalia, the prerogatives and the oppressions of times long passed. The common people simply did not want this sort of life nor this sort of society.

The last years of Louis's reign were difficult ones for Ducange, as they were for any writer who proposed to comment critically upon the contemporary scene. The government was sensitive and determined. Trenchant censorship was established. In Paris troublesome men were silenced; Guizot and Royer-Collard were summarily removed from their lecturing posts at the University. Institutions like the School of Law were peremptorily closed. Restrictions were drawn so tight that even Chateaubriand, the convinced and ardent defender of monarchy came to grief. He who had founded the *Conservateur* to defend and champion the cause of royalism was obliged to submit his writings for his own newspaper to the suspicious eyes of a censor. This was too much; he would not bend to this. He left the staff of the journal. Under these conditions it is surprising that Ducange managed to publish the novels he did, *Léonide* (1823) and *Thélène* (1823). And we are not at all surprised to hear him speak of a novel he wrote and then withheld from publication. As it was, *Thélène* got him into trouble and he had to scurry into Belgium to avoid another arrest. He had managed to offend the government once more.

His misdeed was treading upon one of the government's sorer toes. Louis's regime lacked military prestige. The king had been placed upon the throne by the allies who defeated the French armies and, like Humpty-Dumpty, needed to be put back up again upon his throne after Napoleon's sortie from Elba. He had, so to speak, come up to the Bourbon Palace riding on a borrowed horse, and it had been humiliating. Now the government looked about for a way to earn some gaudy but inexpensive military glory—perhaps a small war, some victories to obscure the painful comparisons between this legitimate monarchy and Napoleon's bastardly glories. Then an opportunity came along that looked promising.

The Greeks were in rebellion against their Turkish masters. Their courageous revolution caused worried concern in all the capitals of Europe. Revolutions threatened to undo the carefully rebuilt status quo that Metternich, Talleyrand, *et al.* had labored so hard and skillfully to reconstruct. The sovereigns met in Verona to consult in Holy Alliance. While pondering the imbroglio, they learned that without even waiting for permission the Greeks had constituted themselves an independent state and had even gathered together in an elected assembly. In Paris, the oligarchy decided that France would not intervene to help the Turks maintain their domination but it would certainly not help the Greeks win their freedom. The Greeks, it was clear, were liberal, and Monarchy would not come to the aid of Liberalism. But the uprising seized strongly upon the popular imagination and sympathies in France. Despite the obvious dangers of writing a pro-Greek novel, Ducange published *Thélène or Love and War* (1823). In a prefatory word to the reader, the author swore to the exact truth of everything in it concerning the Greek Revolution.

Truthful or not, *Thélène* was a very bad novel indeed. The hero, a dashing young Frenchman, went to

Greece to fight in freedom's cause, was shipwrecked, met an adolescent princess whose youthful charms included perfect French, a lovely bosom, and the capacity for falling in love instantly. Then, inexplicably, the setting changed to England where hero and friends coached about the countryside. As they travelled, they commented approvingly upon the contrast between the sturdy English yeomanry who were dignified, literate and enlightened because they had a liberal government, and the French peasantry who were quite the opposite because they had not.

The Royalists were most reluctant to dismiss their hopes of martial fanfare and glory; their warlike ardor aroused, they glanced carefully about for another situation that might let them serve both themselves and the cause of Right. For instance, there was Spain, an excellent possibility. Spain was next door and her monarchy was in danger.

South of the Pyrenees, Ferdinand VII had allowed mildly liberal men to conduct his government since 1820, but shortly afterwards he began actively to conspire against them and even called upon Europe's monarchs for help. His piteous cries begged other crowns to remove him from the captivity in which he languished. In Verona, the diplomats now discussed the Spanish Question. France was nearest and her ultra-royalists were eager. She was charged by the Holy Alliance to restore Ferdinand to his rights. One hundred thousand soldiers led by the Duke of Angoulême, husband of the unfortunate Duchess, advanced into Spain, freed Ferdinand from his enemies and won a small skirmish at Trocadero. Now the French royalists had their victory

and they promptly inflated it to grandiose proportions.
There was a *te deum*, a triumphal procession for
the army, feasts, fireworks and parades. They made so
much out of it that the soldiers themselves blushed.
Even the Duke tried embarrassedly to minimize the
affair, calling it a "Don Quichotterie."[5]   Then it was
discovered that a swindling supplier to the French armies
had bilked the government so largely that the war cost
exactly twice the hundred million francs appropriated
for it.   When this profits scandal became known, the
swindler, Ouvrard, gained immediate nation-wide noto-
riety and the Duke of Angoulême became a figure of
national laughter.   The proud, aristocratic Duke had
been duped by a simple swindler, and a commoner at
that.

Ducange could not resist this opportunity for satire.
At least he said he could not. He claimed he wrote a
novel about two sorts of fools: one, a Marquis who was
very proud, and the other a crooked supplier to the
French army. Then Ducange had second thoughts and
changed his mind. Even though already advertised as
"soon to appear," Ducange stopped the novel's publication, telling his readers about it only in the foreword to
his next novel, *Léonide*. There he explained that he had
already spent six miserable months in prison because of
the Duchess and did not want to risk more months because of the Duke. This was why he cancelled the novel
and doubtless why its replacement, *Léonide,* was as uncontroversial as it was, a simple love story that could
offend no one. The author's caution was praiseworthy
but too late. *Thélène* saw print and the Ministry of War
saw *Thélène*. Someone in the war office read the novel

and found it tainted with Bonapartism. Proceedings against Ducange were instituted. Afraid, this time, of more severe punishment, Ducange hurried into Belgium and returned to France only after Louis's death brought Charles X to the throne. During the first months of the new king's royal magnanimity he was able to have the charges against him quashed.

Except for these early months, the seven years of Charles's reign (1924-1830) proved difficult ones for Ducange as for many other writers. The trouble was Charles and his anachronistic views on royal prerogatives. He bragged that he was the only man whose ideas had not changed since 1789. Rather than govern in a limited monarchy like the Kings of England, he would prefer to be a humble woodchopper.

With such a mentality guiding it, Charles' reign became one of more severe political and social repression. Ducange published only four novels during his reign and of them only one dared criticize the regime, *Isaurine and Jean-Pohl or The Revolutions of The Castle of Devil's Rest* which appeared in 1827. A badly disorganized novel, it first sketched the lives of various occupants of a medieval castle: the scruffy family of crusaders who built it, the royal mistress married off to a man glad to accept the gift of a chateau along with a pregnant fiancée, and finally the bourgeois family of the Revolution who bought it and turned it into a prosperous paper mill. Having taken some seven hundred years worth of steps backward in order to get a good running start toward the present, the novel finally told the unimportant story of Gustave, the handsome, virtuous son of the protestant mill owner and of Isaurine, the lovely daughter of a returned noble family of émigrés.

All ended happily. Ducange's theme was also familiar: the church of Rome was a fatal influence upon the nation because it relied upon threat and terror to dominate the Catholic faithful and keep them in ignorance. The Protestants had all the better of it from Ducange who saw them as self-reliant citizens whose religious ideals were also worthy social principles which encouraged industry and democracy.

Accompanying the by now quite familiar portraits of Ducange's malevolent noblewomen and evilly plotting Jesuit priests and his railing against ancien régime institutions was an evident note of fatigue. Bickerings between liberals and ultra-royalists had become of less and less importance to him. Such quarrels had earlier stirred Ducange to bitter energy and copious rhetoric. Now, he was tired, and because he was, he turned a weary disillusioned eye upon his own life and career. He was forty-four and still obliged to earn his living as a writer of melodramas and cheap, if timely, love stories. Reluctantly, he allowed his memory to wander back into his own past and gingerly consider the not too many years he could reasonably expect to live. What, indeed, did a man of his age say to more naive readers, who, themselves, were in full flight towards escape and hope? Should he tell them the kind of lie that was so easy to tell? That life became more and more glorious, that right conquered wrong, and that they would all certainly live happily ever after? This was the sort of falsehood that both young and old wanted so desperately to believe, if only for a moment, and to hear repeated, like children at their bedtime story, just once more! Or was it better to tell the truth as one saw it, even if viewed through eyes that blurred out of wistfulness and regret? Ducange hesitated, then decided to risk the truth. Hopes and regrets, almost the whole of life was composed of these two things. Men rocked themselves to sleep with the illusion that everything would be fine later on, that they had to hurry to attain some imaginary goal. So men ran, did not attain their goals and then stopped, out of breath, disillusioned and disgusted. Their youth spent in chasing youthful dreams, middle-aged men (children that they still were) invented still other dreams and rushed out in frantic pursuit of them. And when it was all over, where was the man who had dreamt dreams? The very word revolution meant a turning and a returning. As Ducange put it:

> The revolution is over; I think that means that
> it is complete, seeing that in making the large
> circle we've come back to exactly where we
> started.[6]

From Bourbon monarchy to revolution, to Republic and Terror and then through Empire only to return to Bourbon monarchy again. Ducange was sore at heart.

His last two novels were written just after Paris underwent two separate street rebellions, in 1830 and 1832. The first of them brought an end to the reign of a French king. Charles X was sent packing.

It all began because Charles had never understood that he could not turn back the clock. But he was right about one thing: his ideas had not changed since 1789. In a speech he read from the throne in 1830 he minced no words in telling his Chamber of Deputies that he expected from his subjects only blind obedience. Even the Deputies objected, so Charles dissolved the Chamber, called for new elections only to discover that the new group was far more liberal and adamant than the old. Again, he dissolved the Chamber, muzzled the press and called for still more elections. But by now, the upper class had had enough. While Charles and his family amused themselves at chess and while his prime minister was having a vision of the Virgin Mary who assured him of the essential safety of the situation, the bourgeois were barraging all of Paris's working people with propaganda, money and arms. Egged on, angry working men gathered in the streets to discuss the affair and ended by overturning carts and prying up pavingstones to make barricades in the streets of the capital, an old, popular pastime in Paris.

Three days of fighting in the blockaded, narrow streets were enough to place the city in the hands of the revolutionaries. Too late Charles tried to abdicate in favor of his grandson. Already placards were appearing in the streets proclaiming the virtues of Louis Philippe. Crowds before the Hôtel de Ville saw Louis stand upon a balcony to receive the ceremonial kiss of approval from the grand old liberal, Lafayette. Charles scuttled out of Paris in all too unkingly fashion, leaving the government in the hands of surprised men who had not dreamed of winning another chance so easily.

It is these three Paris "days" that formed the setting for the climactic scenes of Ducange's *Marc Loricot or the Little Chouan of 1830.* Though it was published a full two years after the event, the novel gave every evidence of having been all too hastily thrown together. Comic and sinister episodes alternated aimlessly in a story that had as little psychological and motivational accuracy as a Marx brothers' movie. The best that could be said of it was that it was, in some sort, a crude redoing of *Candide* transferred to the political level. Marc, a young seminary student in traditionally devout Brittany, ran away only to be unwittingly entrapped in a Congregationalist plot to stage an ultra-royalist coup d'état in Paris. He was enrolled, given secret documents, promised a huge reward and sent off to Paris. The novel was formed of the events—and they were many!—which befell him along the way. Events helped him to change his innocent mind so that when he arrived in Paris, he switched political sides, joined the workers at the barricades and thus helped to topple the government of Charles X. The little rightist had seen the liberal light.

For all its flaws, the story was a rousing and entertaining one. Over the whole book lay the high good humor and energy of a restored Ducange whose male delight in the detailing of feminine charms was matched only by his thunderings against the Church of Rome. Once again, the hero was handsome as Adonis, the heroine a veritable marvel of enchanting innocence and firm fleshed promises. The reader found himself upon pleasurably familiar ground.

Ducange's last novel used Paris once more as its setting, Paris during the "days" of June 4th and 5th, 1832. Once more rebellion roamed the streets of Paris. But the reasons for it stemmed directly from the outcome of those earlier days of 1830. While the workers who had toppled Charles' government stood happily and triumphantly atop their piles of pavingstones or milled joyously in the streets, their high hopes were dashed. Even as the poor rejoiced, the new governors gathered their briefcases and busily prepared to assume leadership. The same oligarchy had done no more than change its figurehead. Charles had ignored the rules of their game so they had got rid of him. These men were the bankers, the professional men, the bond-holding property owners and industrialists who simply wanted to defend the rights their fathers had won for them in 1789.

The new regime, of the same old landlords and capitalists, chose a new king who personified their economic doctrines. Louis Philippe was a bourgeois king, representative of a society that was changing, albeit slowly. No longer was France a triangularly shaped society whose base was the people, whose midsection was the aristocracy and whose pinnacle was the king. Nor did the whole of this triangle form, as it had earlier, a Gothic spire pointing heavenward from where God bestowed power to rule. Now the triangle of society was a misshapen one. Its base was still the people, but the midsection bulged in solid, bellylike bourgeois fashion while the spire was blunted, foreshortened to make a dais upon which the King—no longer King of France, but King of the French—sat in comfortable superiority. Not too near, but still within reach, Louis Philippe was an excellently chosen bourgeois king.

Parisian workers were not long in discovering that they had been used, manipulated cynically and skillfully by the wealthy and the powerful; they had been the cat's paws for a class that had no intention of bettering the lot of the poor. Their resentment at the role they had been duped into playing during the Revolution of 1830 expressed itself in several spontaneous outbursts in 1832. Several times they again took to the barricades, but they were ruthlessly put down. The National Guard, manned by determined and well-armed bourgeois did not hesitate to shoot to kill.

Ducange placed his *Joasine or the Priest's Daughter* in the very midst of the June rebellion of 1832. For once, his hero, Alexis, was not a dashing lower-class Frenchman, but a young Polish noble. In all other respects he was as the popular novel's hero had to be: brave, impetuous, handsome and courteous. Incredible ups and downs brought him to the barricades where he fought alongside the Paris workers, sharing their humble sausage and bread. With their food and wine Alexis also drank in a warm appreciation of the virtues of the working classes. Joasine, the heroine, resembled all her fictional sisters closely enough; she was fifteen (except when Ducange forgot and made her sixteen), had dimpled arms, a tiny waist, in sum, the usual collection of richly enticing contours. Ducange stopped to point out appreciatively that Joasine's bosom jiggled and joggled and tended to overflow her bodice.

Now a new figure drew the author's attention: the young Parisian worker caught up in the resentments and hatreds of his class and time. He was pictured most sympathetically as he hurried to take his place in the street fighting. As before, Ducange allowed himself copious comment. Yes, he advised his worker ironically, go running out to give your blood and your life for things you would not even begin to understand. Yes, go ahead and die for liberty. If bullets spare you, the gallows are waiting for you and the very people who pushed you into fighting will be sleeping peacefully in their beds.

In his final tale, Ducange's angry and energetic railing against old enemies dwindled; he was no longer the militant writer. His anger had turned to bitter, amused cynicism: the last refuge of a disappointed liberal. His attention wandered into literary annoyances. Almost pettishly he noted that Racine and Voltaire had been dumped into the wigbox of outmoded styles to make room for new writers, Sainte-Beuve and Victor Hugo. But Hugo, he observed with a flick of malice, overstepped the bounds of the permissible. His *Marion Delorme* had shown nobles behaving in too unflattering a fashion; that was why it could not be presented during Charles's reign. Ducange recommended a modicum of prudence. He had learned the lesson for himself. One should not speak ill of the gods nor say nasty things about the grandmothers of living duchesses.

Then death interrupted the writings of this oddly engaging man. Only a few fragments of stories and fewer essays remained to be published posthumously. But in them, as if he knew he had not much longer to live, Ducange made an effort to sum up what he knew and what he felt. It had been a long and demanding life for him just as it had been for the nation. There had been so much: regimes changed so often, wars won, wars lost, and France ended by returning to the very monarchy it had spent thirty years trying to escape. And for him, too, there had been more to do than he had been able to accomplish: a living to earn, a wife to support, injustices great and small to protest as well as the varied cruelties that men worked upon each other. How to decry all of this? What good had he done with his cheap novels and his loud protests, his evil Jesuits and implacable, conspiring duchesses?

He had begun his career, writing popular literature with all the courage of ignorance. He had learned to grin ruefully at his own naïveté: the Restoration government struck hard and with a well-mailed fist. But he had not disavowed his politics nor ceased to express them. Once and for all he had chosen not to return to an irretrievable past but rather to live in the present. Finally, men had to see through their own eyes. In his writings he had described the social and political truths of his time as he had perceived them. Through the exaggerations of his stereotyped villains and heroes he had mirrored the interior life of a people sore beset. He had shown the fears and ghosts and daydreams of the populace. Perhaps now a smiling stoicism was, after all, the best if not the only possible attitude a man could take when he looked down upon life from the lonely promontory of old age. Sooner or later, France would have to acknowledge in her politics as in her literature the existence of her people. Possibly France would even learn to take strength from this ignored majority who ever more audibly insisted upon a present of their own because of the future it implied.

CHAPTER IV

Gestation of a Hybrid 1820 – 1830

→→ *DURING THE DECADE OF THE 1820'S, THE POPULAR LIT-*
erature tightened its hold upon its own audience but
scarcely seemed to cause any stir among the well bred.
Yet, in reality, much of importance was taking place.
The popular novel and the melodrama were slowly working their influences upon public taste, and, even more
important, upon two writers of genius.

The popular novel continued to flourish among the
working classes, treating, as has been seen, contemporary
events and contemporary struggles and using characters
chosen from the unconsulted majority. But well-bred
readers were obliged to wait until the turn of the decade
to read Stendhal's *The Red and the Black* which abruptly
spurned the Restoration's genteel tradition of muted,
formalized love and offered instead the life and passions
of a peasant youth. The same public had to wait until
1833 before Balzac's *Eugénie Grandet* detailed the realistic imprisonment of a provincial heiress.

In quite similar fashion the melodrama continued

61

its brash triumphs among the working classes but required almost all of the decade to effect any perceptible change upon the respectable theater. True, in 1827, in a youthfully arrogant preface to his play, Cromwell, Victor Hugo proposed to do away with the unities of time and place and to enliven the theater with a grotesque mixture of tragedy and comedy, the whole bathed in some sort of effulgent local color. This, of course, was what the melodrama had been doing all along. However, theatergoers had to wait until 1829 to see Dumas's historical drama, Henry the Third and His Court, to be able to appreciate what melodramatic techniques could accomplish. A year later when Hugo's Hernani touched off the famous battle between literary conservatives and the young romantics, it proved, among other things, that the melodrama had been taken up and enthusiastically embraced by the respectable theater. But, again, it had taken a decade for the popular literature to make its imprint.

The imprint upon Balzac in Paris was made directly. Even though his own family had not been able to bring itself to applaud his first literary efforts, a classically oriented drama in five acts of dismally uninspired verse, he was still determined to become a writer. He looked about the current literary scene. What was in fashion? What was selling? Not only were the sentimental novel and imitations of Scott making money for their authors but those crude comic and sinister novels were having an even greater success. If others could imitate and make money by doing so, why not he? Balzac threw himself into deliberate imitation of all the modish literary products of the day, hoping to imitate their financial success as well.

One by one, he tried to find the recipe for success from Scott, from Maturin, from Pigault-Lebrun, from Ann Radcliffe and from Ducray-Duminil. In 1821 he published the *Heiress of Birague* modeled after Mrs. Radcliffe and *Jean-Louis* combining Pigault and Duminil's effects. Then, in 1822, *Clothilde de Lusignan,* an historical novel in the manner of Scott, next *The Centenary,* a sinister novel following the Englishman Maturin's *Melmoth* and finally the *Vicar of Ardennes,* Balzac's respectful bow in the direction of the sentimental novel. Not one of these painful imitations pleased the public.

Thus the decade passed before Balzac, poor in pocket but rich in the literary experience of his imitations, began to write the novels that found a public in large part precisely because they incorporated the lessons he had learned. In 1831, he published *The Magic Skin,* in 1832, *Louis Lambert,* and in 1833, *The Country Doctor* and *Eugénie Grandet.* Clearly Balzac now possessed his writer's craft. What, now, was his debt to the popular literature? What had he learned? Where, exactly, had he learned it?

These questions are the more pertinent because for Balzac the novelist's craft was just exactly that, a skill, a trade to be learned. There was no question of artistic temperament or of inspiration. A writer either knew his trade or he did not. Honoré Balzac, ever since his earliest imitations published under an anagram of his name plus an undeserved but flattering noble particle Lord R'hoone (Honoré de Balzac) had wanted to be a professional writer. Through incredible labors he became just that. Later, he is supposed to have explained that he had worked from a plan in his imitations. "I wrote seven novels just as one studies: one to learn dialogue, one to learn description, one to place people in groups, one for composition. . . ."[1] The process was doubtless not so orderly as the remark would have us believe, but a comparison of Balzac's techniques with those of the popular novel proves immensely fruitful. There are many important similarities only the first of which is that of social milieu.

Balzac dealt with French society as he observed it directly during the Restoration and the July Monarchy. In startling contrast to the usual sentimental novel, Balzac depicts not just a monied nobility but many classes: the returned émigrés anxious to recoup their lost fortunes through marriages or through shady political manipulations, the rich bourgeoisie, puffing as it ran after the elusive prizes of fortune, consideration and honor, and the petty bourgeoisie, the shopkeepers as well as the servants, coachmen, shopgirls and laborers. For long the popular novel had done just that. Earlier it alone treated the woes of the little people, the loves of a peasant soldier, the day-to-day life of the majority. This new milieu he took directly from the popular novel.

The same workshop also gave Balzac a time—the present—in which to situate his novels. Too much has been written elsewhere of this writer's stated goal of being "the secretary to his own time" to require an elaboration here. It need only be pointed out that, while well-bred novels sketched a vaguely ancien régime setting, the popular novel and Balzac's located themselves squarely and deliberately in the contemporary moment.

But Balzac took more from the popular novel than the time of his settings and the milieu of the lower middle and lower classes. Its influence was much more pervasive than that. Maurice Bardèche has it that "the only literary genre whose charm upon Balzac was permanent was the sinister novel"[2] and its by-product, the melodrama. The explanation for this continuing influence is that the young novelist learned important parts of his craft from it. The lessons he absorbed gave him a number of literary techniques and devices he continued to make extensive use of even later as a mature professional novelist.

The melodrama set before Balzac a model he could follow, a model of simple and brutal action, violent passions and tragic confrontations. In addition it showed him how melodramatic effects could be stacked one upon another for increased effect as well as the time-honored popular theater custom of having as brilliant and striking a last scene as possible. The melodrama made quite unabashed use of the "fatal peril" to arouse its audience and dearly loved to maintain the tension until the very last scenes in which the peril was removed by a marvelous salvation. Balzac took this technique and improved upon it; he saved the hero or heroine from one danger only to deliver him or her into a worse one.

Another technique he learned and then perfected was that of creating the melodramatic mood. The tone, the dialogues, the atmosphere of imminent peril and of hidden dangers which boulevard theaters had so lovingly cultivated were all present in the bourgeois dramas that Balzac, with heavy flourish, uncovered for his readers. Even though he changed the setting from the melodrama's shepherd's cottage or lonely hut deep in the forest into a well-to-do provincial household or the Rue St. Denis, he kept the unmistakable mood of the melodrama. At a certain moment in his novel, the lights dim and curtains open, as in *Eugénie Grandet,* upon a terrifying action, a tragedy. The drama was bourgeois, perhaps, lacked poisons, daggers or bloodshed but it remained triumphantly melodramatic. His penchant for these theatrical devices remained a permanent part of his novelist's arsenal. In *Father Goriot* (1834) and even in *Splendors and Miseries* (1844) he still made camouflaged use of these tricks to get a character out of a difficulty or to bring on another wished-for crisis.

His lessons did not all come from the sinister novel and the melodrama. The other popular theater, the vaudeville, was also there to offer still another source of technical help to the would-be writer. Both the comic novel and the vaudeville taught him much.

Both genres used situations and people who were very far from what the well-bred reader found in his polite novel. The characters were not noble; they came from the bourgeoisie or from the people. What is more, the social level of these vaudeville figures had nothing at all to do with the grandeur of their passions or with the depth of their misfortunes. Since everything was treated for its potential for comedy, the spotlight of attention was aimed closely but good naturedly at certain types. There was the spindly-legged country squire, the good-natured chambermaid, the male clerk in the milliner's shop with pretentions to refinement. This gallery of comic characters, observed with a keen and satirical eye, offered encouragement to Balzac's growing fondness for creating types: the doting father, the miser, the ambitious young man from the country. He found in the comic novel's vaudeville, just as in the sinister novel of the melodrama, models of a freer, richer humanity to draw.

He grasped and welcomed the freedom of the popular literature, the varieties of alternatives it offered in place of the vapid respectable literature. It is unthinkable that Balzac could even have imagined writing seriously about the heartbreaks of a retired spaghetti manufacturer without his apprenticeship in the workshop of the popular novel.

In imitating and pursuing the possibilities of this lively unselfconscious literature, Balzac discovered and then went on to explore systematically the immense, untapped substratum of French society. Without this "find," the *Human Comedy* could not have been written. In Balzac the sinister novel, the comic novel and the novel of manners all fused into the novel of the bourgeois and of the people. Realism in literature took a great step forward.

The second of the realistic literary geniuses upon whom the popular literatures were working their influences was a man who also chanced to spend the same decade in Paris. Unlike Balzac, Henri Beyle (or Stendhal) was no stripling when he arrived there in 1821. He was thirty-eight, had fought in Napoleon's armies and had preferred to live in Milan rather than return to France to live under a restored Bourbon monarchy.

But harrassed by Metternich's Austrian police who suspected him, quite correctly, of liberalism, he returned to Paris where he found himself in a difficult position. He did not have enough money to live as he would have liked and he dearly valued his access to many of the important Parisian salons. There he could maintain and even embellish his favorite posture as the well-travelled man of wit and taste. His solution, like Balzac and like Ducange, was to try to earn money by his pen.

He was not totally without experience in writing: he had published in Milan in 1815 a *Lives of Haydn, Mozart and Metastasio,* had followed this by a *History of Painting* that was all too obviously full of plagiarisms and then by *Rome, Naples and Florence.* None of these works brought him the consideration he sought, much less the money he needed. He spent six years in Paris before he published his first novel. For several of these years he wrote as a journalist reporting to readers of various English journals upon the state of French Restoration fiction. He evidently read widely for he found occasion to comment not simply upon the well-bred literature but also upon the popular novel and novelists as well. He mentioned and even recommended Ducange's stories to his English readers while admitting their lack of art. Lamothe-Langon, author of *Monsieur le Préfet* (1824) and other harmless concoctions, made a lasting impression upon Stendhal, lasting but negative. In the margins of his unfinished *Lucien Leuwen* Stendhal reminded himself to "give something human, some real details" to his characters. Otherwise they would be no more than the "simple mannequins" of Lamothe-Langon. Clearly one popular novelist furnished Beyle with a model, if only of what to avoid!

Another popular novelist who made a somewhat better impression upon him was the comic novelist Pigault-Lebrun. In 1839 Stendhal began his attempt at a comic novel. It portrayed provincial Normandy and had all the earmarks of a Pigault novel: pretentious or grotesque ancien régime nobles, a priest who mounted the pulpit to frighten his flock by invoking a fantastic hell and for main character a bearded hunchback who laid seige to the hearts of the local great ladies. The novel was not completed; it is perhaps just as well. But what more natural and lacking in surprise than that Stendhal turn to authors familiar to him when attempting a venture into what would have been for him a new field. *Lamiel* lay unfinished and unpublished along with *Lucien Leuwen* until after his death. His first published novel, *Armance or Scenes of a Parisian Salon in 1827,* appeared in that year. It caused no stir at all. If he had hoped to capitalize upon the timeliness of his subtitle, he was disappointed. But the title did make clear that he was writing of the present and of social circles he claimed to know well. The novel itself also announced that Stendhal was a writer who understood these times and who belonged to the political opposition. *Armance* was the acutely observed story of a young nobleman whose sexual impotence paralleled and symbolized the social impotence of the whole of French nobility. Octave, the hero, was clearly the last of his race. The writer's daring lay in making such a comparison so openly. Despite this boldness the novel did not succeed.

Stendhal offered his next manuscript, *The Red and the Black,* to the printers in 1830. Again a subtitle of marked interest: "A Chronicle of 1830." Once more he was writing of the immediate present but he had widened his scope. No longer limited to the small *précieuse* world of Parisian salons, he proposed to enlarge it to take in all of France. Moreover, the novel was vehemently political. Beyond any doubt, the author was a curmudgeon.

He seemed to denounce the whole of Restoration France. Ultra-royalists and liberals were flailed just as stingingly as the flippant bored aristocracy. It seemed that this angry novelist had deliberately set out to give his well-bred readers a whole series of unnerving shocks. First, he presented as his hero an out-and-out peasant youth. By all respectable literary standards of the day, peasants were not the stuff of which heroes were made. Next, he showed his Julien as a devoted worshipper of the whole myth of Napoleon. One could hardly have chosen a personage more upsetting to the sensitivities of his readers. Then Stendhal had his disabused hero become the lover of not one but two ladies both of whom were irrevocably superior to him in social station. The first was a member of provincial gentry and the second the daughter of a peer of France. Upward mobility via milady's bedroom was not at all what the Bourbon Restoration proposed to encourage. Finally, throughout the novel readers were given a horridly unpleasant picture of France as Julien (and Stendhal) perceived it: a France suffocating under the rapacious hands of the nobles, the rich and the church of Rome. Those readers who finished the novel were permitted only one small satisfaction. They saw how the governmental system protected them from upstart peasants. The novel ended with the execution of Julien.

Without undergoing such deliberate and direct influence as had Balzac, Stendhal nonetheless brought to the writing of his own novels both the time and the hero of the popular genre. He absorbed the lesson of contemporaneity which the ill-bred literature had long been offering. Both novelists had learned from it. In addition, the influence of the popular literature flowed into still another area, that of the drama. There it powerfully influenced the two men whose dominance of the Romantic theater is unquestioned.

Alexander Dumas and Victor Hugo owed much to the lowly melodrama. Critics may argue whether the one or the other created the Romantic theater. Was the battle of *Hernani* an event of greater or lesser literary importance than the success of Dumas's *Henry the Third and His Court*? The question is moot; both men were marked for life by the popular theater. Since Dumas's play appeared first and since critics agree that the play contained the beginnings of the historical drama, the national drama and the modern drama, it is only just that attention be given to Dumas's extensive debt to the theater of the boulevard, and to Pixérécourt in particular.

Dumas's dramas resemble those of the father of melodrama just as did those of Caigniez and Ducange. These resemblances are not at all surprising. Like thousands of other Parisians Dumas frequented the theaters of the boulevards where he too felt the irresistible impulse to join in these heady successes. Evidently the evening when Dumas saw the famed actor Frédérick Lemaître and the adored Marie Dorval play in Ducange's *Thirty Years or the Life of a Gambler* was a memorable one. In his memoirs he spoke of it almost lyrically. Understandably, when the lyric moment had passed, envy set in. Dumas, like so many others, set about to discover the formula for success upon the stage. For six years he applied his mind and his explosive energies to learning how to construct a play, a melodrama. He learned well but learned just one pattern.

An examination of his plays, whether the early *Henry Third* (1829) or his later *Tower of Nesles* (1832), shows that his approach did not change. And it was precisely the formula of the melodrama. Easily recognizable were the melodramatic penchant for impressive settings, the now familiar characters, the deliberate ups and downs in place of believable action and a happy willingness to abandon verisimilitude. All these constitute the maker's stamp of the popular theater.

Like Pixérécourt, Dumas dug into the treasure trove of past French glories, battles and triumphs for his settings. Earlier, Pixérécourt had thrilled audiences with his *Siege of Nancy.* Now, in 1829, Dumas enchanted audiences with the intrigues of the royal court and still later with the flamboyant mysteries of the *Tower of Nesles.*

Dumas shared Pixérécourt's taste in the characters they moved to and fro on the stage. Indeed Pixérécourt had fathered the foursome of the dramatis personae that the Romantic theater legitimized: the young girl, gentle as an angel, proud, tender, valiant and pure; the young hero whose soul was transpierced with mystery and love; the thoroughgoing villain or traitor; and last, the fourth character varying from servant to uncle to husband even to father, who provided relief, humor and good sense. Both dramatists unabashedly preferred as heroes men who lived upon the very fringes of society: dreaming idealistic bandits, crudely sketched Robin Hoods. Pixérécourt's Victor was an early proof print of later Antonys, Buridans and Hernanis. Even in their heroines the two writers were much alike. Pixérécourt's heroine, Coelina, the child of mystery was in reality the daughter of a fine lady. It took only one more short step to make her the daughter of a prince or even of an executioner.

Finally both authors were equally bold in their stage techniques, or rather, in their reckless disregard for these niceties. Neither hesitated to open a play with a shocking seduction scene nor, if either felt it called for, to end a drama with a veritable bloodbath of mass murder.

Dumas faithfully followed the lessons he learned from Pixérécourt then added his own huge talent for bravura writing and found himself applauded and esteemed. Among his literary colleagues who envied him there was the young Hugo, also hugely talented and vastly ambitious. One can easily understand Hugo's envy. Well before Dumas, in 1827, Hugo had written his *Cromwell* only to have its performance forbidden. Charles X was rather touchy about plays that dealt with royalty in any but a respectful fashion. So Hugo had written a resounding preface to his play and had had it published instead of produced.

The well-bred public took note not of the play but the preface. For those who sided with the Romantics this preface gave an engaging analysis of societal history to prove that freedom in the drama was an historical imperative. For the embattled conservatives of literature it was an infuriating irritant, a first shot in the impending battle that was to rage about the premiere of Hugo's *Hernani* only three years later. But for all its engaging qualities which still beguile anthologists into reprinting it rather than the *Cromwell* it was written to introduce, the plays of Hugo, not his prefaces, are still the important thing here. One must consider the product, not the advertising that accompanies it.

In Hugo's plays, from his *Cromwell* (1827), *Hernani* (1830), *The King is Amused* (1832), *Lucretia Borgia* (1833), *Marie Tudor* (1833), *Angelo, Tyrant of Padua* (1835), *Ruy Blas* (1838), to the final resounding failure of *The Burgraves* (1843) there exists a body of material quite voluminous enough to show the essentially melodramatic nature of all of Hugo's theater. Two points seem vital in considering this material.

First is that all of Hugo's plays were improvisations. They were written in great haste very much as were the boulevard melodramas, thrown together from that great mass of proven situations, confrontations and imbroglios that had "worked" before. Only by borrowing all too freely and at times frantically could he have produced *Hernani* in one month's work, *Marion Delorme* in one month, *The King is Amused* in three weeks, *Lucretia Borgia* in eleven days, *Marie Tudor* in three weeks, *Angelo* in a month and *The Burgraves* in five weeks.

The second point to be considered is the sticky one of Hugo's borrowings from his competitors. To put the matter baldly, Hugo copied freely from the successes of others, less matter for dishonor or disdain then than today. The melodramatists of whose works Hugo made free use were themselves no less guilty nor more innocent. Their works too had been the result of a selective, magpie-like snipping of a scene here, a situation there, a likely bit of dialogue to be picked up and carried off for later use. A glance at the chronology of Dumas's successes and following Hugolian dramas seems convincing. Dumas's *Henry Third* was played and proclaimed a success and just a few months later Hugo's *Hernani*, well advertised and well claqued, provided the occasion for the famous literary battle which no student of French culture need be reminded of. Common to both plays was the extravagant use of medieval local color, the familiar popular theater foursome of dramatis personae, the penchant for striking scenes, spectacles that cried out to be painted.

On May 29, 1832, Dumas's *The Tower of Nesles* appeared; in February of 1833 Hugo's *Lucretia Borgia*. The similarities are inescapable. Marguerite and Lucretia, incest and the mother, the mother and incest, feasts and orgies in the tower, feasts and orgies in the Negroni Castle, cadavers in the Seine, and cadavers in the Tiber. True, Hugo turned the roles around so that in his play it was the son who killed the mother, but he kept the accessories, the masks, the daggers and the poisons. The same is true of Dumas's *Christine* (1830), and Hugo's *Marie Tudor* (1833). Hugo's *Angelo* followed a bit too closely upon the heels of Dumas's *Catherine Howard*. But the real significance is not the specifics of Hugo's debt. Rather, the important aspect of it all is that Hugo's dramas were melodramas. They were so in content, in form and in method of construction. His best plays rise above this level but only by virtue of their language. His worst fall even below the level of melodrama. They fail because they lack the melodrama's saving grace of action even when totally unmotivated.

As the decade of 1820-1830 ended, the popular

literature might, like some seasoned artisan of a humbler craftman's guild, pause from its work to consider what success it had had in ten years of dealing with pesky but gifted apprentices. In the field of the novel, Balzac had been clumsy, a difficult one to teach. But he had stuck to it, tried hard and eventually had learned the lessons he had been offered: how to draw characters, master dialogue, solve an obstacle, or prolong the action with unexpected twists. And, of course, he had learned to widen the scope of his story to include people of every class and profession. Stendhal, too, had learned this, but certainly the teaching had been less direct. It was more difficult to assess the degree of the popular literature's influence upon him. If he had not been influenced, it was certainly not due to lack of exposure to the same models. He had read cheap novels by the dozens, had recommended some of them to English readers and had even reminded himself to avoid certain of their errors.

But in the drama, the success of the artisan's literature had been immensely greater; here it was almost total. Both Dumas and Hugo were melodramatists by nature as well as by their evident schooling. Apt pupils, they had adopted, even improved upon almost the entirety of the melodrama: its technique, its situations, its personae and its conventions.

The popular literature had exercised a surprising influence upon both respectable genres, the Romantic theater and the sober, contemporaneous novel, during this apparently unpromising decade. Now the 1820's were over and the decade of the 1830's was just beginning, the decade of youth for the new literary hybrid.

CHAPTER V

Further Adventures of the Popular Literature
1830 — 1840

→→ *POPULAR LITERATURE WAS SEGREGATED FROM THE RE-*spectable until the early years of the 1830's. But early in the reign of Louis Philippe, the distinctions began to fade. Romantic drama borrowing the crude strengths of the melodrama won its victory with *Hernani* and thus gained access to almost all Parisian theaters. Under its own name or that of Romanticism, melodrama was able to go where it wished in the city. Similarly the well-bred novel took advantage of a certain easing of censorship to expand the subjects and the people it treated, thereby greatly widening its own audience. Now novelistic realism commenced its stroll through the lower levels of society, observing with eyes freshened by new interest.

Whether the phenomenon was one of well-bred literature tolerantly slumming or vulgar fiction climbing the social ladder is not, for the moment, a question that requires solution. What is important is that boundary lines between the two literatures were less and less observed over the ensuing years. This was true to such an extent that by 1840 it was almost impossible to tell one from the other. The two were merging under the compelling pressure of the most banal reason, money. Every author wanted to increase the size of his public and, as a consequence, his income.

The drama of the thirties embraced melodrama for the simple reason that it was good business to do so. And, as we have seen, it was a fairly uncomplicated process by which Romantic drama earned money while the melodrama acquired its *droits de cité*. But, for the novel, the process was a bit more complex since it depended upon the coming to fashion of a new journalistic device, the *feuilleton*. From humble beginnings, the feuilleton would gain such popularity that like a tail suddenly wagging the dog it would take predominance over the newspaper that carried it.

Physically, the feuilleton was no more than a folded insert in the newspaper. It added to it, very much like the magazine section of today, brief literary reviews, society notes and fashion items. Smaller in format, it was freer from the attentions of the censor and much more timely than the official pronouncements that made up the majority of the columns of the paper itself. It excited the same sort of interest that gossip columns and advice to the lovelorn attract today.

The appeal of this little insert became even more important when, after 1830, French editors, copying their English brethren, halved the cost of subscriptions and counted upon increased circulation to make up the lost revenue. Publishers tried various changes in the content of the insert to attract new subscribers. One such device which now has its own secure place in French journalistic history was that of publishing works of fiction chopped up into segments of convenient length. The first such was a translation of the Spanish *Lazarillo de Tormes* which appeared in the August 5 issue of the *Siècle* in 1836. This highly episodic tale of inventive rascalry lent itself well to installment publication precisely because each episode was short enough and self-contained. Thus began the history of the printed continued story.

The *roman feuilleton* as it was called succeeded and came to dominate the feuilleton itself as well as the journal of which it was only a part. One chose one paper rather than another because of its serial; editors fought over and paid highly for novelists whose writings attracted an ever increasing readership. Daily circulation figures reflected instantly the reception the public either gave or withheld from the serial. René Bazin speaks of the paper whose press runs varied, in the first week of a new serial, from 50,000 to 80,000 according to whether the public liked the tale or not.[1] When we consider that the *Constitutionnel*'s number of subscribers rose from 3,000 to 40,000 when it signed Eugène Sue to write its serials, we begin to understand the dimensions of this new, popular sort of literature. But, then, all of journalism was becoming a much more lucrative affair. The inducements of the lowered subscription rates and a serial sent subscriber lists soaring. "From 70,000 in all of France in 1836 (the year of the debut of the serial) the number rose in 1846 to 200,000 for Paris alone."[2]

With such popularity, the newspaper serial could not hope to escape criticism. Perceptive, conservative literary critics joined in lamenting what the brilliant but prissy Sainte Beuve termed "industrial literature." The term was not ill chosen: editors hired, quite understandably, writers whose prose succeeded in pleasing the greatest number. Failure to do so was punished by instant loss of revenue. Critics quickly understood that such novels could not meet the standards they wished to develop for the novel as an art form. They saw that such writings must, inevitably, reflect more and more the concerns and the taste (or lack of it) of the masses. These critics deplored and then bitterly attacked the sad situation that placed the novel in such unworthy, slipshod hands. Their displeasure is understandable; accustomed to the gentilities of the well-bred octavo novel and obviously uninformed about the popular subliterature, they viewed the rapid change in kind and quality of printed fiction offered them by the feuilleton as a degradation of their own respectable novel. What these critics did not at all understand at first and came only slowly to understand later was that these newspaper serials were popular because they attracted the audience which the duodecimo novels of the lending libraries had formed. The very same classes and sorts of people were now reading in cheap newspapers the stories they had found enchanting in rented, two-sous-per-day hardbound volumes. What the critics were witnessing without realizing it was the popular novel's simply changing vehicles to get to an enlarged public.

This was the reason for the popularity of the serials. Well written or not—and they were not!—these hasty, primitive cliff-hangers were precisely what the large public wanted. Like T.V. soap operas of today, many, many people followed them.

And, as with the Parisian melodramas, the vast public was not composed solely of the lower classes. At the height of its popularity the feuilleton (for example, Sue's *The Mysteries of Paris*) held both plebe and patrician enthralled.

> Old Marshall Soult, President of the Council, he too seems to live only for the sake of the sacramental words, "the rest tomorrow." Anger, despair if the story is interrupted . . . the minister bursts into his office one morning, an air of catastrophe; a governmental crisis? The Minister collapses into a chair and moans: "La Louve is dead."[3]

A few glances and a few details suffice to prove that the *roman feuilleton* is indeed the popular novel we have known. The characters: Dagobert, or Robert or Jean-Jacques, the old soldier under Napoleon; Fleur-de-Marie, the virtuous if slightly soiled working girl; the Count d'Auray driven by greed and ambition; Rodin and d'Aigrigny, both evil Jesuit priests. Of course a lovely and persecuted heroine was required and was always present. She was lusted after by a heartless wretch: Gontran de Lancry, Viscount Scipion. And protected by an honorable hero: Paul Jones, Rodolphe. Shadows of Ducray-Duminil and Victor Ducange—the familiar types of the duodecimo novel are instantly recognizable.

The skills and the techniques of the feuilletonist are also ones we have seen before. René Bazin sketches them.

Serial writers, almost all of them, have an exact sense of dramatic movement: a science of the horrible and of the terrifying; a skill at unravelling the skein of human motives; a skill at leaving for dead, on the battlefield of the action, heroes who come to life for a lengthy destiny: an adroitness in the use of suspension points: a fidelity to . . . good mothers, hard working shopgirls and eternal loves. . . .[4]

And the recipe for writing a good serial? Not too difficult as Louis Reybaud explains it:

Well, sir, you take, for example, a young woman, unfortunate and persecuted. You add a bloody and brutal tyrant, a sensitive and virtuous page, a confidante who is sly and perfidious. When you've got in hand all these people, you shake them well together . . . and you serve them hot. Each installment has to fall right, so it is linked to the next one by a sort of umbilical cord, so it appeals. . . . Let's suppose that you have a certain Arthur whom your public is drooling over . . . at the end of each installment, there is a critical situation, a mysterious word, and Arthur, always Arthur at the very end. And if you can have Arthur straddle a subscription renewal, threatening non-renewers with not finding out what happens to the hero, you'll have managed the finest success . . . that a man of style could hope for.[5]

Yet there is no mistaking it. This was the very
same novel. It had simply changed vehicle, its mode of
transportation in order to find its way to more people.

Both melodrama and the popular novel found larger
audiences. The novel was able to hop agilely onto the
presses of the newspapers—like Pauline of early installment movie thrillers hopping from ice floe to ice floe—
but the melodrama had needed its face scrubbed and its
language improved a bit by Romantic tutors before it
could be presented to the whole wide world. No matter,
both genres now had the audiences they wanted. Of
more importance is what they proposed to say to them.
Surprisingly, the melodrama found little new to say.
Dragged willy-nilly along the paths that Hugo and Dumas
pursued, it was obliged to lend its strengths to historical
dramas, to Romantic passions until the public finally
grew tired of the excesses and signaled its displeasure
by imposing failure upon Hugo. His *Burgraves* proved
to be the last Romantic fling; it failed in 1843. Melodrama, in company with well-bred Romanticism, lasted
the decade but had not much more of social importance
to say.

It was rather in the pages of the feuilleton that
literature reflected quickly and clearly some of the violent changes in life patterns that the French were being
obliged to undergo. Romantic melodrama must have
seemed more and more old fashioned and finally quite
irrelevant during a decade which saw the introduction of
large-scale industrialization into France. There was
larger use of steam power to run heavier machines in

new and bigger factories. Railroads were planned and built. The novel was much better equipped to deal with these realities now that, for a majority of the French, life was being radically altered, battered by the appetites of a headlong industrialization. The price of economic *laissez-faire* grew steeper. As the decade progressed writers of almost every sort turned their minds and pens to the new problems, the new social ills. Alcoholism, prostitution, malnutrition, labor strikes: these were real problems which had been suddenly and disastrously aggravated by France's giddy rush towards industrial modernity.

Thinkers of all sorts considered their changing society, analyzed it as best they could and proposed all manner of solutions. Some wanted to abolish the rules of capitalism, to return to a Rousseauian commune-like naturism, others sought only to modify the harsher aspects of its economics. Fourier, Saint-Simon, Enfantin, and later Louis Blanc and Karl Marx, all had their ideas. Their proposals differed greatly but all agreed upon the importance of writers. They were vital to reform, social or political, since it was they who had to explain to the masses the ills of society and, more important, the advantages of proposals for change. Writers were wooed. By no means aloof, the writers turned their attention to the present; however, they refused to play the role the theorists assigned to them. Perversity? Perhaps, or possibly because utopias are so very difficult to write about convincingly, but in any case, professional authors rejected the espousal of specific political solutions in favor of illustrating the problem. Here melodrama as well as the novel could function quite ably.

Since the plight of the working classes was at the heart of the problem, the obvious hero was the honest, faithful laborer, the heroine a virtuous starving wage slave, and the villain a banker, factory owner, or money lender. Usually melodrama focused upon a single aspect of the problem. Ducange's *Thirty Years or The Life of a Gambler* had moved and frightened its audiences with the horrors that attend the betting man. Some authors portrayed the evils of drink while others pictured the painful steps along the sorrowful trail which led a virtuous working girl to prostitution. No doubt about it, the spectacles of misfortune were moving; here melodrama could use all its potent techniques. But, to combat the fearful ills of a ballooning capitalist society, dramatists offered solutions that were ludicrously inadequate. Private charity was recommended to answer nation-wide poverty. Young girls were exhorted to die of starvation rather than become whores. The drama, lingering long in describing the ailment, was rather slow in prescribing for the patient.

The novel also took its time about suggesting specific new remedies, but it got there eventually. Authors, like other humans, come only gradually to understanding. One writer who, like Ducange in an earlier decade, both understood his own times and brought this comprehension into his fiction was a literary jack-of-all-genres. Known best as a feuilletonist, the man illustrated and expressed the direction and the progress of the agile subliterature. Significantly, the important part of his career began in 1836, just as the newspaper serial was being introduced. He is an author who, although he is little studied, if at all, today, was, in his own day, a striking literary figure.

A professional writer like Ducange and Balzac, Frédéric Soulié wrote and published more than one hundred volumes of novels and saw twenty-one of his plays produced. He merits analysis and perhaps even reconsideration because of his role in the development of the popular literature. After all it was he who wrote the first feuilleton best seller and became thereby the first king of the newspaper serial.

Little in his beginnings gave any indication of his career to come. The son of a philosophy professor at Toulouse, he studied at Nantes, at Poitiers, and at Paris, then returned to work under his father in a registry office. Provincial clerkdom seems impossibly remote from fame in Paris. But at twenty-four, in 1824, Soulié came to Paris where he spent the rest of his life until his death in 1847. He began his literary career in the capital in traditional fashion, with the obligatory book of poetry, *Amours françaises,* and followed this with two dramas in verse. Unlike Balzac's attempt of the same sort, one of Soulié's plays did have a modest success. But by 1832 Soulié had had enough of literary gentility and poverty. He abandoned literary niceties for more profitable crudity: he followed his ambition into the popular genres. That year he published a historical novel, *The Two Corpses,* and saw his five act play, *Clotilde,* (in prose this time) staged. Both were successes, probably because of his wholesale use of slaughter and shocking scenes.

The influence of the sinister novel and of the melodrama was obvious in *Corpses.* It opened on the execution of England's Charles I and closed with the great fire

of London. In between were crammed the birth of
Charlotte Stuart in gritty, detail, related scenes of
treachery, rape, murder, exhumations and—shades of
Gothic writers everywhere!—the disfigurement of the
already decapitated body of Oliver Cromwell. For
reasons much too complicated to go into here, Cromwell's severed head was sewn back onto his body to be
removed once again. Here is how Soulié handled the
action:

> Having drawn near the cadaver, the would-be
> executioner in whom hatred had, surely,
> stifled all reticence and prudence . . .
> finally kicked the head of the senseless body,
> giving a savage cry of joy. But, under the
> blows of the ferocious executioner, the threads
> which held this trunk and this head together
> . . . tore through the rotten flesh, detached
> themselves completely and allowed to fall, on
> one side, the body which struck the pavement
> with a soft, flaccid sound, while the head,
> restrained for a moment in the flowing knot
> that pressed the neck, seemed to move, to
> tighten and finally also came loose and disap-
> peared.[6]

Soulié strewed the landscape with corpse after
corpse until in Chapter XXII he felt obliged to ask his
readers if they saw any sense in his title of "two
corpses." Then, he answered his own question: the only
really important corpses were those of Charles I and
Cromwell. As for the others . . . well. . . . But the

book had a great success. Between 1850 and 1874, some fifteen editions or reprints were announced. An English critic of his time (1839) gushed:

> This awe inspiring romance . . . written in a charnel house, by the light of those flickering candles that in Catholic countries surround the corpse . . . by an iron pen dipped in human gore, is the most extraordinary creation of the brain that was ever yet . . . presented to the world.[7]

Clotilde, his play, fared well too. With his collaborator Bossagne, Soulié produced a drama that included seduction, robbery, murder and a double death by poisoning. In it, young Christian murdered a rich money lender for his cash. With this he now carried off Clotilde who willingly gave up riches and social position to join her lover. But she who gladly suffered social opprobrium for love's sake began to pine under his growing neglect and finally denounced him. As the play ended they were reconciled in love and died together by poison.

Mademoiselle Mars who played Clotilde must have brought to the title role more than today's reader can easily imagine. It is still astonishing that such a play could have succeeded upon the august boards of the Théâtre Français, the bastion of dramatic conservatism, the tomb of the literary ghosts of Molière, Corneille and Racine. Only three years had passed since Hugo and his claque had imposed victory for Romantic melodrama at the battle over *Hernani.* Now the inner sanctum itself had been laid bare. Soulié himself understood very well what the significance of it all was and took complacent pride in it. "I state categorically that it took a certain vigor and a powerful skill in the hand which, in *Clotilde,* broke that barrier so happily."[8]

The play itself lasted for several years on various French stages. It was revived in 1840, and in 1843, most fittingly, at one of the old homes of the melodrama, the Porte St.-Martin theater.

Emboldened by those two successes, Soulié plunged wholeheartedly into commercial literature. Journalism, short stories and three more novels brought him little literary credit or money. However, one of these novels, *The Councillor of State* does merit our attention because it represents an important step in the career of the first important feuilletonist and because the novel itself moved the newspaper serial towards serious social concern. Its thesis was that a virtuous woman was defenseless when confronted by the corruption of Parisian society. The book in brief summary unfolded thus:

Camille, by her beauty, character and education attracts and marries Alphonse de Lubois. Alphonse, depraved by an evil actress, attracts attention to his misconduct which Camille learns about when she hears a chance remark made by Maurice. Maurice, remorseful at wounding Camille, tries to ward off and save Camille from a whole series of disasters that come her way and which are all traceable to the corrupt hypocrisy of Parisian society. Repeatedly, she must either persist in virtue at the price of social disgrace or abandon virtue, embrace hypocrisy and gain social respect. Finally, when Camille has lost friends, reputation, suffered financial ruin and been deserted by her heartless husband, she surrenders to her fate and gives herself to Maurice.

Here was a novel which, although neither serial nor duodecimo, nonetheless addressed itself to a contemporary problem, which dealt understandingly with its heroine-victim and which indicted society. Soulié disclaimed any effort to draw a moral from his story; rather, he limited himself to showing that only the totally cynical manipulator was rewarded. Both the virtuous person and the insufficiently hypocritical scoundrel were doomed.

This was a strong stand by a commercial writer who had to please his audience. But more was to come. If we stop to comment upon the novel it is because only a year later Soulié became the first widely-read serialist and the first of these to criticize his own society as an enemy. For the moment, Soulié used no sensationalism to sharpen his attack upon the injustices he saw. This came, though, just one year later in 1836 with his famous and savagely dramatic feuilleton, *The Devil's Memoirs.*

This curious best seller, now totally lost from literary esteem, appeared in installments over a two-year period from September, 1836, through January, 1838. Three different papers, the *Revue de Paris, La Presse* and the *Journal des Débats,* shared in the burden and in the profits of this incredible novel. *Devil's Memoirs* was then and remains today almost unbelievable in its length, its complexity of plot and the number of its interwoven subplots. When published in book form, as it was shortly later, it required eight volumes in octavo! Set in France in the 1830's, the book launched a savage attack upon French society of the Restoration. In Soulié's *Councillor of State,* Camille, the virtuous woman, was the victim of male Parisian hypocrisy and vice. *Memoirs* expanded the condemnation to denounce a whole world in which, as a matter of normal course, virtue was exploited and persecuted while, still as a matter of course, vice triumphed with the aid of cunning.

The basic device of the book was that of a man who made a bargain with the devil. Armand-François de Luizzi bargained, at the risk of his own soul, that the devil must recount to him the life story of anyone whom Luizzi designated. The devil's stipulation was that Luizzi must listen to the whole story or else lose one month of his life. Luizzi shrewdly bargained that he might write down and publish all the devil's tales. Since Luizzi wrote them down as the devil told them, Luizzi served as the devil's secretary and his writings were, as the title indicated, *The Devil's Memoirs.*

These stories constituted some four-fifths of the book and unvaryingly illustrated Soulié's thesis of a world turned upside down, where vice reigned and virtue suffered. Humans were either hunted or hunters, victims or villains. A rich and esteemed banker got his start, one discovers, by robbing his own father. A worthy magistrate married his own daughter to silence her. She was the proof and fruit of his incestuous love for his own sister. Tale after tale of vice, hypocrisy, misfortune and human perversity, but not tales told in file, one after another. Rather they were intertwined, interwoven, the one begun only to be halted while another was advanced and in turn interrupted to finish an earlier story. Such was the complexity of the action and of the narration that Soulié required some nine chapters of denouement to bring all the stories to an end and to tie up all the loose narrative threads.

Luizzi's death, when finally it came, greatly resembled that of Tirso de Molina's Don Juan. The period of his bargain having come to an end, Luizzi took fright and tried to escape paying the devil his due, but he was too late. He tried to pray to God, but, "as he bent his knees, as he placed his hands together to pray, a bell sounded and a resounding voice exclaimed, 'the hour for choosing has passed, Baron, follow me!' "[9] Like Don Juan, Luizzi was swallowed up by the earth. So ended the book, but before bringing this enormous ship of fools to port, Soulié had told dozens and dozens of stories, had created a veritable labyrinth of intersecting subplots. Perhaps one story, its strands gathered together from the many installments, and restitched together here, will give a small sample of the melodramatic doomsday timbre of the work.

A young noblewoman consents to marry the lover of her Countess mother. Her marriage so distresses one of her former suitors that he takes orders and becomes an exemplar of piety until, in an absent-minded moment, a prostitute gets him drunk and debauches him thoroughly. So thoroughly in fact that he resolves to become just as wicked as he had been pious. With the aid of his priestly function, the natural piety of the young wife (in name only) and some drugged wine, he

succeeds in seducing her. The young marquise drowns
her own remorse in wine and commences to alternate between alcoholic lubricity and penitential piety. Luizzi
happens upon her during one of her lubricitous phases,
enjoys her favors and errs by bragging lightly about it.
Sober now and sorry, the marquise learns of his remarks
and is so ashamed that she flings herself from a window.
The devil enlightens Luizzi about the consequences of
his chance remark.

But Soulié's devil was not always of the sort that
dragged Don Juan to fiery hell; this novel had neither
the intent nor the tone of religious diabolism. On the
contrary, Soulié's Mephisto was sophisticated, urbane
and only slightly fearsome. When Luizzi first saw him,
he was in dressing robe. He sat down to smoke, tilted
back his chair and began to hum a tune. Luizzi addressed
him in an inflated, bombastic manner saying "Son of
Hell, I have summoned thee. . . ." The devil interrupted him and remonstrated smoothly:

> First, my dear fellow, I don't know why you
> call me, "thee"; it's very bad taste. I'll point
> out to you that in calling me "Son of Hell"
> you are just mouthing one of those stupidities
> that seem current in every known language.
> I'm no more the son of hell than you are the
> son of your own room just because you live
> there.[10]

This devil was very much a man of the world of
men. Cynical and all powerful, he was of a piece from
start to finish and functioned as the author intended

him to do. He was Soulié's vehicle, his means to an end and that end was social satire of the bitterest sort. The world of this devil and of Soulié was a hateful and hurtful one. Obviously, Soulié felt himself roughly used by it. Openly disabused and quite sincere, he addressed himself to his readers in his preface.

> Do not come to Paris, young man, if you cherish ideals of love. In Paris the woman you worship on your knees . . . will be treated lightly by men you despise. If you try to write nobly of beautiful things, the public will laugh at you and the critics revile you . . . you will find, as I found, that the public will be impatient with anything you offer that is not sensational. Unless you accept the demands . . . you will be obliged to live in poverty and obscurity; and if, like me, you are unwilling to forego the warmth of popularity and the comfort of money, you will yield to public demand. You will sit down, as I do, and you will write on a sheet of paper the *Memoirs of the Devil*, and you will satisfy a vicious age by a picture of its own vice.[11]

Soulié himself had taken the devil's coin of the feuilleton and having made the bargain to produce a steady stream of installments was in the horrid position of a man strapped to a printing press. He had, willy-nilly, to write his stint or the machine threatened to swallow him whole. This was industrial literature with a vengeance. Out of this entanglement came many of the flaws that marred his writing so. He was guilty of all the faults that frantic improvisation could entail: loose and careless construction, obscurity, complexity and heaviness. Despite these usually fatal flaws, he was adroit at manipulating a complicated plot and proved that he knew how to bring his narration to life. Withal, he was a writer who seized his readers' interest. He was even able, when the goad pricked him sharply enough, to put his very exaggerations and violences to effective use in his outbursts of angry resentment. At times, he almost succeeded in raising vituperation to the status of a respectable literary art.

He possessed an undeniable energy and even a certain dash. Doubtless these qualities helped his novel to succeed because it did have a prodigious success. It was reprinted several times in French, translated into German, Spanish and Italian, and—a high though unorthodox accolade—was pirated repeatedly by Belgian printers. More important, the novel became the talk of all Paris. The first widely popular serial was having a considerable influence.

One obvious effect of its popularity: it led to a spate of devil pieces in the theater, fiction and essays that was slow in drying up. In the theater alone the record is convincing. In 1842 the Vaudeville presented *The Devil's Memoirs,* and as late as 1849 the Gaieté offered *The Devil's Bell,* and during a three-month span in 1844 not less than six devil productions were simultaneously offered to eager Parisian audiences.

But more important influences were those that Soulié brought to both the form and the content of the feuilleton. Useful as the serial was in increasing a paper's circulation, the appeal of the story was less than maximum so long as one day's installment did not whet the reader's interest to read the next. One answer to this problem was Soulié's trick of interrupting one story and turning to another in the course of a single issue. With interest aroused in the first story then diverted to one newly begun, how could the reader not wait impatiently to buy his next copy of the *Journal des Débat's Devil's Memoirs*? If today's readers smile too indulgently at this old fashioned trick, let them think just once more of television's soap opera before pronouncing judgment. In any case, the feuilleton was vastly popular, and it was precisely this that brought on another problem.

How to keep the story going without stretching too far the naive credulity of readers? The trick was, of course, to include within the plot of the story the machinery necessary to allow for its indefinite continuation. One had only to build in at the very beginning of the novel a situation that would permit an almost endless piling of story upon story. Certainly, this solution was not new; it was as old as the *Arabian Nights,* as the *Canterbury Tales.* In Soulié's *Memoirs* there was the devil who was obliged to tell the whole life story of anyone Luizzi chose. (Soulié's devil required, we remember, that he be listened to throughout the whole story.) The possibilities for continuation were virtually endless. This device was one worth saving and using again. In later feuilletons Soulié did just that. In *Unknown Dramas* a house, number 3, Rue de Provence, provided for the telling of the histories of all those who lived in it as well as those of all their friends and their enemies. In *General Confession* a whole series of confessions centered, more or less, about the determining of who Noel's father was. In *If Youth Knew* an old man has his youth and his memory restored so that he can live life again while knowing what he had learned the first time. He could simultaneously recount his second life and stretch it out with memories and stories of his first one. Possibilities for continuing, if not endless, were clearly adequate to last the lifetime of a most devoted reader. Simple changes, simple tricks were what Soulié brought to his feuilleton, but tricks so useful that others copied them, and the serial flourished because of them. But there were other changes too.

The content of *Memoirs* announced the entry of the popular novel into the newspaper serial. Stories distinctively characteristic of the cheap duodecimo volumes of the provincial lending library now began to appear in installments in newspapers. The popular novel changed vehicles and did so with an amazing speed. Only five weeks after *Le Siècle* published the first work of prose fiction as a feuilleton, *La Revue de Paris* began to publish Soulié's corrosive condemnation of French society. Like the hardbound popular novels, *Memoirs* dealt with contemporary society, spanned several classes and illustrated, albeit simplistically, social injustices. Satire and social criticism now made their appearance in the serial.

Not every continued story was henceforth a novel of social concern. Many would be historical romances like Dumas's *Three Musketeers*, others would be pastoral novels, still others, particularly under Balzac's pen, would be sober examinations of contemporary French life without condemnation or cry for change. Still, *Memoirs* set a

pattern which lasted as long as the feuilletons themselves. It was in the columns of the serialized novels that
popular writers of social conscience made their views
known. The explanation for this is twofold.

First, serialists now had available to them a hugely
increased audience. Earlier, social criticism in the popular novel was widely read but reached only those working-class people who could afford a few sous to rent the
books and get to a library to do so. With the cheap press
of the dailies now easily available, the working-class
audience was greatly swollen and to it was added the
thousands and thousands of middle- and upper-class
citizens who fell prey to the charms of this literary
novelty.

Second, the injustices the novelists wrote of provoked increasing response among readers of all classes.
Soulié's bitter attack came at the very moment when
society was under attack from several other quarters.
Political theorists and economists like Saint-Simon and
Fourier examined society, found it woefully lacking and
said so loudly. A theologian, Lammenais, compared
society with the precepts of Christianity and trumpeted
his biblical prophecies and calls to action. Many
thoughtful men were coming to agree that the unequal
distribution of wealth was an injustice of unhappy
fertility. Unjust itself, it also created other vicious social
ills. Though they disagreed upon the solution to the
problem, they agreed that the poor, the unenfranchised,
the workers and peasants were the victims. They also
began to agree that sweeping reforms were absolutely
needed. Soulié's novel provoked strong response.

If Soulié was the first immensely popular serialist,

he was far from alone in his search for public favor and quick fortune. Many others tried to hawk their hasty literary wares in the columns of various newspapers; most of them have long since found the oblivion they clearly deserved. But it is interesting to see that Balzac, driven as always by ambition and his constant need for money, began early and wrote tirelessly for the feuilletons. Indeed, so compelling were the prospects of being widely read and of finding financial ease that the feuilleton earned a grudging, tacit sort of literary respect. By 1840 even respectable writers were happy to sell their pens along with their superior sensitivities in this marketplace. Musset, Lamartine and even the king of the literary realm, Chateaubriand, wrote for the installment press. Their reasons for doing so are most understandable: books were considerably more expensive than the cheap press, readers were increasingly shunning the prestigious octavo format and instead were devouring their daily dose of vicarious escape in the newspaper. The feuilleton was new, rich and important.

For a short while, until 1840, Frédéric Soulié reigned unchallenged over this newly formed kingdom. It was he who first, in *Memoirs,* caught and held the attention of a vastly enlarged audience. His writings, timely and critical, captured the interest of the public. Like some popular singer of today, he rode the crest of their interest and rose to fame upon it. He gave voice in his columns to uneasy stirrings of conscience that were shared by a growing number. Government, its bases? Its very purpose: whom should government serve and what are its responsibilities? These questions were signs that a long, slow and painful process was in motion,

the democratization of France. The popular serials of
social protest would now begin to play a large, even a
commanding part in this slow growth towards social and
political justice.

And as the feuilletons played this part in the world
of actuality, they also asserted by their very existence
that a similar process of democratization was painfully
under way in the smaller, more tightly governed realm
of literature. In 1839 wealthy bourgeois of the political
right could still, for a few more years, reject the notion
that the poor should have the same rights as the rich.
From the literary right, critics could still deplore the
sorry sullying of French literature by the vulgarities and
crudities of this "industrial literature." Nonetheless,
both politics and literature in France unmistakably felt
something stirring there upon the horizon.

CHAPTER VI

The Last Adventures of the Popular Literature
1840 – 1848

→→ *PUBLIC FAVOR, SOULIÉ SOON DISCOVERED, WAS A DISAP*-pointingly fickle mistress. His intimate liaison with her lasted little more than a year after the last of his *Devil's Memoirs* in 1839. Not that he did not hope fervently to keep her. Of course, he tried to repeat *Memoir's* success with three more long, intricately-woven, panoramic novels cast from the same mold: *General Confession* (1840), *If Youth Knew* (1841), and *Unknown Dramas* (1845). They had a certain popularity, but now Soulié no longer reigned supreme.

Favor did not so much abandon him as oblige him to share her with other writers. For a while, until 1842, this creature of whim hovered, undecided, among several serialists and then, with disconcerting swiftness chose her new gallant. What sort of feuilletonist did she choose? Not, certainly, chubby Balzac who puffed and sweated in his grim, relentless pursuit of her. His appearances in the feuilletons were becoming more and more frequent, but the public still had to get used to his

101

lumbering ways. She chose instead a handsome, wealthy wastrel of a dandy who affected yellow gloves (thrown away after one wearing), who demanded the very finest in horses and carriage, yet who came to insist that he was a socialist. Like most endings, it all came about very simply. Frédéric Soulié was displaced by Eugène Sue.

The first installments of Sue's *The Mysteries of Paris* appeared in the *Journal des Débats* on June 19, 1842. Thereafter and for sixteen full months, this serial overshadowed almost every other event of French life. Once again, fiction presented itself to life and, believed by the living, received the very gift of life. The ups and downs of its characters took on a far greater importance to those who read it (and those to whom it was read aloud) than the actual events of real life. Everywhere in France its success was sudden and complete. But incredible as was the reception the public lavished upon the novel and its author, both had had their own preparations for this quick catapulting to fame. The man himself was nearly as fabulous, in the strictest sense of the word, as his novel.

Eugène Sue, born January, 1804, was the son of a wealthy doctor, one of a long line of hard-working and successful doctors. Despite energetic rebellion, Eugène himself finally submitted to paternal pressure and became a medical man, serving as medical officer in the French navy and with the French armies that invaded Spain in 1823. But he was a doctor with a difference, a physician whose ambition it was not to be one. He dreamt only of living in Paris. There, with enough money to spend, a man could go to the balls, dance, drink, flirt, be seen and see all Paris that counted. For Sue, this was the only life worth living.

In Paris, at twenty-six, with his appetite for spectacular living freshly whetted, Sue had no means of supporting himself. He certainly did not intend to practice medicine. Luck arranged it that he inherit a fortune. In the same year his grandfather and his father both obligingly died and left him what they had worked so long and calculatingly to amass. He was immensely rich. Instantly he resigned his commission in the navy and commenced to live the existence of the well-to-do dandy, dabbling in literature as he dabbled pleasurably in all the excitements of Parisian life.

To be young and wealthy in Paris during the first months that followed the July Revolution was to be defiant. One showed one's defiance and contempt for Louis Philippe's stodgy bourgeois regime by a tireless show of haughty impertinence and by calculated extravagances. One acquired a loving expertise in the finest horses and the newest carriages to show off at Longchamp, that modish promenade. Insouciant, one drove one's own coach and four through the crowds at carnival time, shouting in racy slang at the bedraggled poor who blocked the narrow streets. One went in search of amorous adventure to every masked ball, to the opera to try one's luck among the dancers. In short, one was young, combative, lustful and given to vast arrogance and cynicism. Sue was all of these.

One could also brave bourgeois conservatives in the literary arena. Battles there always had strong political overtones. What delight to affront the established philistines in saucy articles or with an essay titled, "OF

IMPERTINENCE considered in its rapports with morality, religion, politics, the arts and literature." Sue enjoyed the literary world, published two longish stories ("Plik" and "Plok," 1831) that were popular and, despite his self-appointed role as man of the world, became increasingly interested in the realm of letters. Balzac, whom he met and came to know very well, encouraged him to write. James Fenimore Cooper, visiting Paris, dined with them both and gave Sue, if only by his example, an idea. Cooper and Scott had made profitable use of exotic settings for their yarns. The one, Scotland, and the other, the mysterious forests of North America. What might Sue have to offer by way of exotica?

Why not the sea? He had come to know the ocean all too well during his tours of duty as a naval doctor. Sue wrote a sea story, *Atar-Gull,* followed it with several others, and found himself hailed as the creator of the sea novel in France. Still the dandy, still very much the gentleman who sought to do all things well but to show no effort in the doing, Sue was pleased with his seafaring novels and grew even more pleased as he considered what he had done. Later, of course, he saw it all very clearly.

> In attempting, as I was the first to do, to introduce seafaring literature into our language . . . I tried in *Kernok* to emphasize the pirate, to give his prototype; in *The Gypsy* to give the prototype of the smuggler; in *Atar-Gull* the slaver; in *The Salamander,* the merchant mariner.[1]

He had arrived in the well-bred literary world. As his reputation among the respectable public grew, so did his friendships with his fellow writers. He and Balzac became close friends; they consulted together, advised one another on ideas for novels and shared plans on how to succeed in the cliquish struggles of the literary world. One of Sue's letters to Balzac shows by its carefree vulgarity the very easy terms of their friendship.

> You are a terrible wretch, you in Paris, not to have said a word to me, not a single word. Do you want to make amends for your ignominy? Ask me to lunch with you, to dinner, to supper, to roam the streets . . . anything you'd like to do no matter how foolish. . . .
>
> Vimont, the publisher, really has a hard-on for you, to the point of blood. If I had had to help him with it to get it started, I would have done so, but, fool though you are, you know very well that the erection occurs at just the mention of your name. So see him, he's an excellent guy. If you think him worthy of allowing him to earn millions of pounds [by publishing you] go ahead.[2]

When he wrote these cheerful familiarities, Sue was still carefree and immensely rich, or so he thought, whenever he deigned to think about money at all. Paris living had given him that ineradicable snobbishness which consisted of studiously ignoring the cost of things while being passionately attached to the opulent luxury money can buy. Then, suddenly, Sue was broke, deeply in debt. He had 15,000 francs and owed 130,000. He had gone through two fortunes as well as the money his writings had brought him. Worse, he found that he could no longer write even the feuilleton he had contracted to produce. He had agreed to provide *La Presse* with *The Diary of An Unknown Man* but could get no further than sketching in the very beginnings. Evidently, he had learned Soulié's trick of building in at the very first of the story a mechanism to allow for its indefinite continuation: the unknown man, a postillion who could tell his own adventures or else recount stories he had heard. But Sue's pen went dry. After the first two installments, he could write no more. His abrupt poverty was clearly the cause of his writing difficulties just as it was the reason for the deeply wounding slights he received from many of his former friends. Confidence gone and totally disheartened, he took the advice that a wise friend urged upon him. Leave Paris and its distractions for the quiet of the countryside and return only when he had finished his serial.

The advice was excellent. Installed in his rural retreat, Sue cast about energetically for topics to write about. He succeeded in publishing a variety of books and articles. A book on horses—Sue, now poor, made thankful use of knowledge gained when he was an active member of the swank Jockey Club of Paris. He also began work on a *Naval History of All Peoples of the World from Antiquity till the Present*. The years 1839 and 1840 were busy in the country and seemed to propitiate the vengeful gods. Sainte Beuve, the important literary critic and Sue's friend, wrote an article on the seafaring novels, praising them, and awarded him the

honor of having first risked the French novel upon the
open seas. Even better, Sainte Beuve appraised the various set pieces Sue had done and lauded the accuracy with
which he painted several contemporary figures, in particular the young elegants, the jaded "fashionables." Perhaps in answer to this encouragement, Sue returned to
work upon a novel of manners, *Mathilde or the Memoirs
of a Young Woman.* It appeared in the feuilleton of *La
Presse* on December 22, 1840, and continued for some
nine months.

The story is of interest on several counts. Its
decided success was great enough to irk critics who
scorned its literary worth. The question of the nineteenth century, as one disgruntled critic put it with
heavy sarcasm, was no longer the to be or not to be of
Hamlet, but rather, what had become of Mathilde. Had
she wept? Yet the novel had several virtues. It went
straight to the roots of a malaise that permeated Louis
Philippe's monarchy. It pictured an apathetic aristocracy—one thinks of Stendhal's treatment of languid
young nobles—with its sudden storms and resulting
panics, instinctive noble scorn and resistance to bourgeois philistinism including its exemplar, the bourgeois
king himself. But this novel was different. If Mathilde,
the heroine, accepted without question Restoration
society, had no doubts about the viability or desirability
of legitimate monarchy, its hero, Albert de Rochegune
was quite a different matter. Inheritor of a great name
and a great fortune, he nonetheless realized the new
needs of his changing society, became involved politically as nobles seldom had of recent date, and took political
action upon the side of democratic liberalism. In this

novel, nobles could be heroes if they understood their own time and acted accordingly. Readers liked to see nobles learning democracy.

The book had other traits that linked it unmistakably to the sinister novel and to the melodrama as well as to the developing newspaper serial story. *Mathilde* contained abduction scenes, noctural pursuits, poisonous bouquets of flowers, drugs-which-allowed-one-to-have-his-evil-way-with-women. All of these were familiar events in the popular fiction. In addition, there was an all too recognizable style, with its "my blood froze in my veins," "a sudden fear flashed like fire through my mind," and its "curse you, Gontran, . . you have killed my child upon my very breast."[3] If one added to these family resemblances the serial's technique of false anticipation—"But let us not get ahead of our story"—to tease the reader and increase suspense, the evidence of kinship was not just convincing but overwhelming. The psychology of *Mathilde* was as might be expected; in its world, people were good or bad and, for the solace of its readers, good always had to triumph over evil.

Mathilde represented a stage, a midpoint between the octavo seafaring novels that Sue first wrote and his feuilleton *Mysteries of Paris* that appeared in 1842. The serial novel was evolving as the principal and most effective voice of social concern, and Sue was undergoing a similar evolution from an attitude of total unconcern with social ills. His slow turn from haughty dandyism to vehemently sincere concern and even a strident demand for social reform has its own importance. It requires noting as an important part of the preparation whereby Sue became a nationally and even internationally known fighter for democratic change. Earlier Sue had treated the prototype of the slaver, the smuggler, the naval officer. Now he assigned to them a moral value, a color even if only one of two choices, white or black. Not, one might observe, a very large step into the kingdom of morality. But it was a step, nonetheless, and only one of several that led Sue far from where he started.

The next step has been told so often that its truth fades almost into the myth of his life. It was Sue's conversion to socialism over a dinner table. Familiar though it may be, the story requires retelling here. Briefly, Sue was taken by one of his literary friends, Félix Pyat, to dine at the home of a worker. Sue was so impressed by the virtuous simplicity of the family, their lack of affectation and the evident good sense of his worker host in suggesting socialistic answers to the problems of the day that, in taking leave of him, he cried out, "I am a socialist." Had Eugène Sue really changed from insouciant dandy to tenderhearted, humanitarian socialist? The story sounds so patently false, so arranged, that one's lips immediately form a smile of disbelief. Yet, as Pyat affirms, it was true.

It all began when Pyat and Sue met during the intermission of the premiere of Pyat's play, *The Two Locksmiths,* May 25, 1841. They discussed the desperate and shocking portrayal it gave of the working poor. Sue was ignorant of such things and quite skeptical. What dandy would not be? To prove the truth of his staging, Pyat invited Sue to dine the very next night with a workingman whom he knew named Fugères who lived on the Rue Basse-du-Rempart. Pyat's talk with

Sue must have moved from the question of workers' poverty to a discussion of their intelligence and political awareness because the Fugères household did not at all illustrate grinding poverty but rather sensibly modest conditions. This was a metal worker, foreman of his own small plant, and he moved briskly despite a wooden leg–he had lost his own to the gears of a machine.

> Sue got out of his brougham, with all the elegance he was still the arbiter of, gloved, polished, glossy, a perfect dandy. He found himself in front of a man in a worker's blouse, sleeves rolled up upon two bare arms and two hands dirtied or rather blackened by metal dust.
>
> The introductions finished, our host asked us for five minutes to change clothing and soon came back to us with white shirt and clean hands that shook our own warmly. He led us from the workshop into his own rooms. There, his young wife, adorned as a true Roman matron by her two jewels of children greeted us cordially. She gave us our seats at a spotlessly clean table, an immaculate tablecloth . . . already served with soup and some beef fit to tempt all Sue's epicurean companions.[4]

The food pleased Sue very much, the conversation of his host even more and doubtless the novelty of the whole affair played its part. In any case, Sue took his leave of Fugères greatly impressed, and in the enthusiasm of his gratitude and his courtesy exclaimed that he was now a socialist.

This dinner may have been his political conversion, but no signs of it showed for over a year. The first installment of *The Mysteries of Paris* (*Journal des Debats*, June 19, 1842) showed no trace of the revolutionary democrat to come. The genesis of this *roman feuilleton* —incredible by its length and by its manifest influence— was most unpolitical, a quite prosaic business affair.

The publisher, Gosselin, brought Sue a copy of an English book which made much of the mysteries of London, its slums and the frightfulnesses of lower-class criminal doings. The best analysis of the probable identity of the book Gosselin brought to Sue has been made by Leslie Fiedler in his introduction to Lippard's *Monks of Monk Hall* (N.Y., 1970), xxiii. Its text and illustrations suggested to both men that such "mysteries" done about the Paris underworld might sell nicely. Sue gave the matter solid thought. First there was his immediate need of money and the unavoidable necessity of his earning it now that he had squandered his inheritance. Then he asked counsel from his friend, Goubaux, whose advice to retire to the country to write and recoup had proven so profitable. This time Goubaux advised Sue not to try it. He wrote him:

> My dear Eugène, you think you know the world and you have only seen the surface of it. You think you know men and women and you have only seen and frequented one class of society. There is one thing you live in the very midst of, that you do not see. . . .[5]

In truth, Goubaux was perfectly right. Sue knew nothing about the people. However, not in the least put off by his own ignorance, he decided to do a French version of the English model and with his usual energy and brio began to write the serial that would change him so radically and would also help to change the very government of France.

For a novel so nearly endless as this one—its installments continued from June, 1842, until October, 1843— its basic plot was amazingly simple. Its hero was a mysterious German Prince, Rodolphe. Rather like Superman of the American comic books, he went about Paris righting wrongs, judging and administering justice and generally trying his infallible best to set things straight according to his own lights. The wrongs to be righted were or could be made endless. Even his name, Raoul in modern French, was a reminder of the errant cavaliers who too made their knightly tours of the wrongs circuit doing the right thing. Handsome, with a charm that worked instantly and never failed, strong and supple as a hero should be, elegantly nonchalant, women loved him. To cap it all off, they found in him, as in any proper romantic hero, a melancholy, mysterious and unknowable grief, a strange pallor. Yet he was action itself. Almost like the son of God, he descended into the slums and hovels of the Parisian poor to accomplish his mission of salvation then to return to Gerolstein, his Germanic paradise. Little blasphemy then in seeing the soiled saint Fleur-de-Marie throw herself upon her knees before him.

The villains he struck with his mighty vengeances were as inferior to real men as Rodolphe was superior to them. All seemed distorted either by birth or accident; the schoolmaster had a face horribly disfigured by acid burns, while others were more animals then men: a tiger, a fox, a snake. Some were even named as such, "skeleton," "bulldog," "owl." But punished they all were. Rodolphe showed in his actions both an opposition to currently held ideas of morality and a complete willingness to take justice into his own hands, even to commit murder if it were richly deserved. His punishments, like his rewards, were paternal, those of an enlightened tyrant who saw the plight of the poor with immense sympathy. His answer to the ills of society was a flood of charity for some and poetic justice for others. This feudal lord ruled and meted out absolute justice in his domain, the Paris of the poor.

Sue drew so heavily upon his physical setting and drew its features so clearly that Paris itself became, under his pen as under Balzac's, a living thing. The very city, like some fearsome murky dragon, took on its own life to obey the harsh imperatives of its own existence. Consuming humans for its food, exhaling the flames and smoke of the huge capital, this was no longer the Paris of powdered salon beauties and dandies; this was the Paris of the poor, and, because poor, the Paris of drunks, whores, pimps, pickpockets, assassins, ragpickers and a thousand other scruffy trades by which human beings tried desperately to avoid the gaping maw of the heartless beast. Both parasites and the nourishment of Paris, preying upon others and prey to the city, Sue's characters were as they were because Paris was as it was.

As the novelist came to see it, the prostitute was no more responsible for her criminal debauchery than was the rich man for his ignorant egotism. The crime of the rich was that of ignorance while that of the poor was simply their poverty. Misery alone forced otherwise virtuous people into crime: the Stabber was a criminal but had many virtues, Fleur-de-Marie was poor but not yet criminal. The lives of both were governed by fate which had put them into their environment of misery and need.

In beginning the *Mysteries,* Sue's goal had been simply to interest his readers, to nurture his public, to shock but not to preach. There was not the slightest evidence of his after-dinner conversion to socialism in the columns of his feuilleton. Certainly not a desire to reform.

> We have not hesitated before the most hideously true depictions thinking that, like fire, moral truth purifies everything. Our word has too little value, our opinion too little authority for us to claim to teach or to reform.[6]

Surely a writer could change his political thinking without necessarily changing his way of writing. But, as the novel began to succeed phenomenally, Sue was obliged to keep on writing and now he had to start the research he had earlier neglected so breezily. He not only read the reports that detailed the living conditions of the laboring and dangerous classes of Paris, he also went into the quarters he wrote about. He visited, got to know them and the people they sheltered. He talked to them, smoked, drank and ate with them and in the doing learned some of their strange argot to reproduce

RODOLPHE

dans la plaine Saint-Denis

Rodolphe, the pensive melancholic hero of *The Mysteries of Paris*.

in his installments. But only slowly did he begin to propose solutions to the horrors he had intended merely to describe.

In the first two parts of the novel, those that appeared before November, 1842, Rodolphe's solution to misery was personal charity and for crime, sharp punishment. But after November signs of humanitarian and even socialistic thinking began to appear. Sue was beginning to realize, well in advance of the vast bulk of the wealthy, that private charity could not cope with public poverty. Society, he realized, had to organize itself to provide for the problem. A model farm of Bouqueval received a glowing description in his story. In the fifth part of the novel Sue was becoming an enthusiastic preacher and by the seventh part he was openly and earnestly the reforming moralizer whose pictures of Parisian hell, salted with portraits of a utopian heaven, teemed with exhortations and lectures to the undecided.

The mixture was precisely what French readers wanted. *Mysteries* had a success that is hard to describe and even harder to understand today. Everyone read it, nobles, bourgeois and the people. The public was simply avid. Lending libraries upped their prices.

Understandably, French literary critics were rocked. Every writer and critic read Sue, each for his own reasons. Despite fairly general agreement that the work was badly flawed, Sainte Beuve expressed his pleasure at its success. Hugo, at work on his own version of the same thing, his *Misérables,* read *Mysteries* and praised it. Balzac, tireless competitor that he was, also read it and raged. Soon Sue's success would cause a rupture in their friendship.   From Macon, Lamartine wrote Sue for a favor.

> My dear poet in prose, an indiscreet request;
> could you give me twenty or thirty pages by
> you, an unused chapter, anything signed
> Eugène Sue to be printed by me here in *Le
> Bien Public*, a paper I write for. . . . If you
> can, you would make us very happy and very
> grateful.   You see!   Adieu, admiration and
> friendship.[7]

The most sincere of his admirers came from the very classes he was writing about, the working poor. Finally, their plight was being noticed by someone who cared.   Letters poured in: requests that Sue not let Fleur-de-Marie die—they loved her too much; that Sue tell what was going to happen—they could not stand the suspense; that Sue give help in finding work for several of his readers, or money; that he write more about the Morel family, Sue's symbolically virtuous worker's family.   In the same sort of identification as between film stars and the roles they play, Sue was becoming for the lower classes, if not Rodolphe, someone very much like him.

Little by little, under the press of its readers' interest, *Mysteries* also changed.   It became less and less concerned with the sensational doings of the dangerous classes and more concerned with the daily drudgery of the laboring classes.   Eugène Sue and Rodolphe moved closer and closer together.   For the workers who read him they were almost one.   A glazier wrote Sue to encourage him in his writing.

No one will dare raise his voice against you because you are the Truth and the Truth is God. . . . Persevere, man of good, persevere in your noble but difficult task. There are still many other mysteries to be unveiled. Go on, strike hard, do not fear, the entire world is listening to you.[8]

Sue was their savior; Sue and Rodolphe were truly one now. A poor wretch hanged himself in Sue's ante-chamber leaving this pitiful note: "I kill myself out of despair; it seemed to me that death would be less harsh if I died under the roof of the one who loves us and defends us."[9]

Eugène Sue, the dandy, the bon vivant, now almost deified by the workers, had become a striking public figure of high importance. As might be expected, he became controversial. He was courted and attacked. Political theorists and social thinkers of all stripes tried to enlist him in their service. Would he lend his support and his pen to the Fourierists in their publication, *La Phalange*? Would "this generous soul," this "spokesman for the poor" publish in the workers' paper, *La Démocratie Pacifique*? Victor Considérant adjudged *Mysteries* to be "the most moral book which has appeared in this century," and readers of his paper presented a medal to the "defender of the social classes, . . the promotor of the organization of work." To Félix Pyat who had long been a zealot in the cause of liberalism, *Mysteries* was not just a novel but rather a "socialist epic."[10]

However, *Mysteries* also came under attack and

from a variety of directions. George Sand, despite her own emotional response to the story, considered that the work was badly put together (and it was) and paid too large a ransom to the literary industrialism of the day. This from a fellow professional novelist and feuilletonist! More serious criticism came from the two extremes of the political spectrum. Sue was caught in a crossfire between the French Catholic church and the German economist, Karl Marx. For the church, Sue was horrifyingly communistic. From various Parisian parishes *Mysteries* was termed "scandalous," "infamous," "arch-immoral." He even learned that both he and his book had provided the subject of a sermon in a church on the Rue du Bac.

> Witness, my brothers, this man whose name it would be a crime even to pronounce; he attacks property, he excuses infanticide. He is the Voltaire of the new hordes who prepare in the shadows new crimes and new carnages. He disguises communism under pleasant forms; he wants to come in to your living rooms, your families . . . but, be warned that this reading constitutes a mortal sin.[11]

If the church thought Sue a wild-eyed communist, it was abundantly clear to Marx that he was not. Instead of preaching the enmity of the classes and the necessity of the class struggle, Sue was preaching reconciliation. His idea of virtuous justice was no more than wild dreaming and the idea of Fleur-de-Marie's rehabilitation through repentance had no validity at all in the frame-

Fleur-de-Marie, the slightly soiled saint of Sue's *The Mysteries of Paris*.

work of communist thought.   No, decidedly, Eugène
Sue had not comprehended.

But the novelist, drawn much more by his emotions than by doctrinaire logic, moved steadily to the
political left, while *Mysteries* continued to be very nearly
the only event to fascinate all the French, and much of
the world as well.   There were translations into German,
Dutch, Italian, Spanish, English, Belgian and Russian.
In New York eighty thousand copies sold in just a few
months.

If he took any notice of either criticism, Sue's
answer seemed to be an even sharper anticlericalism in
his next serial and a refusal to accept Marx's convictions
about the inevitability of the class struggle.   As if to
make public his peaceable idealism, Sue bowed to the
urgings of the Fourierist Victor Constant and allowed
him to publish an article of his in the first issue of
Démocratie Pacifique.   Significantly, the paper's manifesto prominently declared that antagonism between the
classes was not unsolvable.   Different social classes shared
common interests which could be harmonized through
union.

By October, 1843, when *Mysteries* finally drew to
an end, Sue had made a fortune for himself and had
also helped, more than any other writer, to politicize
the Parisian working classes, to make them aware of
their common needs and even of their possible strengths.
He had also traveled a large part of the distance that
separated him from a fervent belief in democracy.   This
was a long voyage for the supercilious dandy to have
navigated.

Sue had only to announce the title of his next

serial to have money fall into his hands. Before writing a single word of *The Wandering Jew* he sold it to the *Constitutionnel* for 100,000 francs. The first of its installments appeared on June 25, 1844. Vast in its complications, it meandered on and on and ended some thirteen months later. The *Jew* followed the pattern of *Mysteries*. Sue had found his audience and obviously knew how to write a serial. Again he set his story in the present and gave himself a framework which allowed him easily to continue the story almost endlessly.

This time he used the supernatural to help set up the ponderous structure. The Jew and Salome (the dancer to whom Herod gave the head of St. John the Baptist) were condemned to wander ceaselessly forever. Since wander they must, they devoted their eternity to helping the descendants of the Jew's sister, the family of Marius de Rennepont now living in France and persecuted for having converted to Protestantism. The Renneponts, Sue's symbol of society's injustice and his ideal of civic virtue, were under constant attack from those old villains, the Jesuits, who conspired tirelessly. They plotted to conquer the world by ruse, they would have liked to reduce to nothing all willpower, all thought, all intelligence among the people in order to deliver them, as Sue put it, "brutish and unarmed" to the despotism of kings. The modern Renneponts staved off the Jesuits' attacks, helped by the magic powers of the Jew and the Jewess. Obviously, Sue could continue these dark doings as long as he wished. Just as obviously, the Jew and his consort, persecuted throughout history, now represented in heavy-handed symbolism today's victims of social injustice, the worker and women.

Like *Mysteries,* the setting was contemporary and Paris was its locus. The Rue Brise-Miche served as a center of focus for this new serial just as the Rue du Temple had done for the other. Sue brought into his tale the very real cholera epidemic of 1832 and made of it a cruel weapon in the hands of the rascally Jesuits. The socially admirable and progressive Renneponts versus the ancien régime Society of Jesus with its reactionary political plague.

In addition to wallowing in anticlericalism, Sue also gave clear signs of becoming an outspokenly militant liberal. The plight of the workers and their right to organize to better their conditions was his clearest concern. In his dedication of the *Jew* he spoke of the workers who "silently suffer, asking only for the right to work [and] a regular salary commensurate with their rude labors."[12] The thrust of the long, involved story was precisely that the church had no viable solutions to offer, that only the banding together of the laborers could bring amelioration. Faced with the miseries of modern society but imprisoned still in its own past and pride, the Church of Rome was an anachronism promising paradise in the next world to justify its refusal to help the people in this one. Therefore, Sue's logic required, the people must turn away from the church and convent, symbols of authority, fear and ignorance, and turn rather towards the meeting houses of the Fourierist communes where lay mutual consent, human kindness and shared concern.

The *Jew* succeeded prodigiously, even outdoing *Mysteries.* The *Constitutionnel* doubled its format, increased the number of its columns from ten to twenty and its publisher, Véron, signed Sue to a new contract. Henceforth he would get 100,000 francs per year for fourteen years in return for ten volumes of feuilletons. Again there were delirious accolades from the Fourierists and the St. Simonists, medals struck in his honor, translations into many languages—and again the furious criticisms.

Conservatives understood the political importance of these feuilletons and attacked them mercilessly. Dreadful, this cheap literature with its erotic passages, its calumnies against the clergy and even religion itself, its appeals to the worst passions, these subversive maxims giving dangerous, even fatal, advice to the working classes. What was the world coming to? The world, to answer the question, was coming to Eugène Sue. Sue had helped mightily to make the serial what it now was and in turn it had made Sue what he now was. In 1844 he was king of the feuilleton in a way that no writer ever had been or ever would be again. In his hands the serial novel became not only a way to quick wealth but an immensely potent political weapon. Certainly, he was a skillful opportunist. He flayed timely whipping boys; witness his melodramatics at the expense of the Jesuits, his espousal of the new democratic ideas that Pyat had helped bring him to. Yet Sue had been the one to forge this great social weapon, and a powerful one it was. Its volleys were heard throughout France and even beyond the frontiers.

Of course, conservative literary critics were unhappy with all of this fame. They much preferred the old, segregated literature. Now that the success of the popular had drawn the respectable literature into combat on the dueling grounds of the feuilleton, they saw clearly what had happened. The humble literature had worked a powerful and radical influence upon their own and they deeply deplored it. Like ancien régime nobles snubbing upstart bourgeois, they scornfully pointed out its undistinguished ancestry. Sainte Beuve cackled spitefully that "starting with Restif [de la Bretonne] . . . Sue is on the way to becoming St. Vincent de Paul while passing by Ducray-Duminil."[13]   The monarchist and literary conservative Alfred Nettement harumphed that "M. Sue leaves far behind him the most adventurous eccentricities of Paul de Kock . . . [in comparison] Sue gives Kock the merit of a sort of relative prudery."[14] Even Sue's friend Balzac, dismayed by his own failure to equal his colleague's fortune, wrote to his beloved Madame Hanska to deny it. "I have neither jealousy nor bitterness against him [Sue] nor against the public. Thank God, our rivals are Molière and Walter Scott, and not this Paul de Kock in satin."[15]

Jealous or not, in August, 1844, Balzac's own attempt at a *Mysteries* came out, *Splendors and Miseries of Courtisans,* and in October the first part of his *Underside of Contemporary History,* which was a direct response to the *Jew.* "The moment requires that I do two or three capital works which will bring down this bastard literature." And then, all friendship fled, Balzac discovered that "in Sue there is a banality which allows anyone to read him," even as he admitted ruefully that "the 310,000 francs that the *Mysteries* were worth might just as well have been mine to keep me afloat."[16]   The same year George Sand published *Consuelo,* admitting that she based her heroine upon Sue's model because no other was "as original, as daring, as touching and as poetic" as Fleur-de-Marie. Hugo, meanwhile, was also busy working up his own version of Parisian miseries. It too would be a contemporary study of the Parisian poor. It too would have a framework that allowed for endless continuation. It would also have the same publisher, Gosselin. But Hugo had just been named a peer of the realm by Louis Philippe; perhaps he thought that honor enough. Yet there was no denying the sincere flattery of Sue's imitators, the importance of the popular novel and of Sue's preeminence in it.

In the pleasant weather of July, 1845, Sue finished the *Jew* and went off to rest in the country. He could now well afford to spruce up the small cottage he had in Le Loiret. There he got to work on still another serial, *The Memoirs of a Valet de Chambre*. A bit worried because he feared people might not take to a hero with a lackey's soul, he wrote anxiously to Véron. He was considering changing the title because, as he explained, the beginning was very important in order to seize the reader. In this feuilleton Sue tried to do for country peasants what he had done for Parisian workers in his earlier volumes. In the retitled *Martin or the Foundling* he unveiled the mysteries of the French countryside, but with a difference. Unlike the two earlier serials where he narrated without overly prescribing for social ills, here he permitted himself large dollops of the same anticlericalism and an even more militant Fourierist socialism. This time, Sand, who knew her peasants, was more than a little taken aback. Sue drew such exaggerated, dark pictures. "He sees peasants through a different telescope from me." Then, she added courteously, "perhaps the ones he has seen are as ugly as that."[17]

The year 1846 was not Sue's year. Whether tired of the struggle or simply desirous of enjoying life, he published very little and watched as Balzac, lumbering but totally determined, finally got his triumph. In just this one year, Balzac brought out in serial *The Comedians Without Knowing It, A Criminal Invitation,* the third part of *Splendors and Miseries of Courtesans* and *Cousin Bette.* He was exultant: "My situation at this moment is sovereign. I alone remain more brilliant, younger, more productive than ever."[18]

This was not entirely true; there were much more fecund feuilletonists, Dumas and his collaborator Maquet. Together, in frantic drudgery, the two managed to fill column after column with their historical romances. *The Three Musketeers* (1844) was the first serial of their ten-year-long partnership. Then came *The Count of Monte Cristo* (June, 1844-August, 1845). By working twelve or fourteen hours per day they were even able to keep several different novels going at the same time. *Monte Cristo* was not the only Dumas-Maquet serial during its publication; there was also *The Lady of Monsoreau* and *Queen Margot,* which appeared in different newspapers but in the same year. True (and it explains a good deal), Dumas-Maquet were paid by the line. Dumas found that a bit of dialogue could stretch into a column with marvellous ease.

> Who? asked His Eminence.
> She and he.
> The Queen and the Duke! exclaimed Richelieu.

Yes.
And where?
At the Louvre.[19]

But not all serialists were so dextrous or so mercenary. George Sand was already a professional novelist when she decided to write for the feuilletons in 1845. Her entry into these columns was prompted by the same desire for a larger income that had tempted others. But even so, she was worried. She wanted popularity, she had indeed modeled her heroine after Sue's Fleur-de-Marie and admitted it, but when she came to sign a contract with Véron of the *Constitutionnel* she was nervous. She was paid ten thousand francs in advance but confessed that she did not know the art of ending a chapter with some interesting twist that would hold the reader breathless. More, she knew she was simply not capable of turning out the hasty, careless work that let other writers grow rich from the continued story.

She was also half way through the series of four novels which critics would later term "socialist." Two of them had already appeared in hard cover. Her *Companion of the Tour of France* (1840) had shown with admiration and warmth the mutual aid societies of the skilled masons, carpenters and the like. She detailed the long and difficult years of the travelling about the countryside which was required of the apprentices who sought membership in these groups. For Sand, even before she entered the serials, virtue lay in the skilled hands and peaceable ways of the working classes. *Consuelo* (1842), also in hard cover, was the second of these political novels, and it was here that she sketched her heroine after Sue's original.

The last two of her socialist novels were published in the feuilletons in 1845 and 1847: *The Miller of Angibaut* and *The Sin of Monsieur Antoine*. They had a modest success. Hers was a more reflective style and, consequently, her audience was a more restricted one. But whether in hard cover or feuilleton, her socialism changed not a whit. It was a gentle, even a somewhat poetic, political philosophy. In her fiction as in her own life, love was the answer to human problems, the universal solution. She saw the social problem, the division of the classes and their differing, opposing interests. But her solution to them was one to drive political theorists to howls of frustrated rage. Love, she was sure, could heal all such conflicts. Love between man and woman was what she proposed to bring noble and peasant, bourgeois and noble together. In *Companion* the reader travelled the gentle and softly romanticized path traced by the lovely heroine. The noble Iseult de Villepreux met, slowly grew to know and finally fell in love with the sturdy virtuous carpenter, Pierre Hugenin whom she married. In the *Miller* readers watched the social regeneration of the wealthy Baroness Beauchemont. In love with a commoner, a Rousseau-struck engineer who refused to marry her, she successively renounced position, title, society and wealth in order finally to become worthy of his staunchly democratic principles. Only after her chateau had burned to the ground would he consent to take her to his socialist bosom and educate the young widow's son in a humble country setting that even the author of *Emile* would have found idyllic.

This, then, was the way in which the profound impact of the popular novel upon its well-bred counterpart was manifested. As a result of this cultural cross-breeding, the area which the genre could treat was now vastly enlarged, the manner and techniques of the novel were radically different and its dramatis personae stretched from the very pinnacle of the social scale down to its dirt-caked foundations.

The imprint of the melodrama upon its cultivated cousin, although even more forceful, brought a different result. Romantic theater had won its victory using the weapons of the melodrama, but when the public ceased to favor the typical historical romances, it was the historical aspects which perished and the melodramatic strengths which survived and continued to flourish. Romantic theater came officially to an end when Hugo's *Burgraves* failed in 1843. But the public had not lost its taste for melodrama; it had shown wild enthusiasm for Pyat's contemporary drama, *The Two Locksmiths* (1841). A comparison of the sort of melodramatic doings the public refused and those they frenetically applauded is in order.

Paris audiences inflicted failure upon Hugo's play despite its melodramatic aspects. The play creaked under the burden of an overwrought medieval setting. And while Pyat's juxtaposing of extremes, rich and poor, wicked and virtuous seemed to please them, they found Hugo's hand with it unpleasant.

Even before they saw this juxtaposition of opposites, the audience heard it. As the traditional three blows sounded and the curtains opened, Hugo's stage directions called for a fanfare of trumpets and bugles, drinking songs sung amidst the clinking of glasses. This was contrasted, in portentous symbolism, by clankings "as though a group of men in chains was coming and going."[20]   Then, as eyes became accustomed to the semi-darkness of the setting, the audience saw a bare-footed old woman, chained from head to toe, dressed in a tattered sack and half hidden by a long black veil. She listened to the drinking songs offstage and then herself began the verbal zigzagging the author found so irresistible. "The princes are joyous, the feast still goes on" she intoned, and then, glancing with heavy significance at the other side of the stage whence came the chain clanking, "the captives beneath the lash work from crack of dawn. Here the noise of orgy; there the noise of irons."[21]

The old hag then ceded the stage to the chained men who entered uttering syllables of fatigue to maintain the rimed couplets of this extravaganza in alexandrine verse. The men sat down and commenced to tell each other things they already knew but which the audience need learn to make sense of the play. As the drama clumped along, the audience also learned what readers of today know too, that this play would not succeed. Its contrived archtypal characters, windy but mysterious, seemed all too unreal. Poetry or no, there were much more interesting plays to be seen in Paris. Not at all that the public had lost its fondness for melodrama, nor was it tired of bombast and contrived action. It still welcomed them eagerly. But the public was tired of historical settings and cardboard crowns; it wanted its melodrama contemporary.

Félix Pyat was one of the writers who helped to

satisfy the public demand for melodrama that was up to the moment. The premiere of his shocker, *The Two Locksmiths* (1841), had provided the occasion that led Sue to socialism over dinner with the worker Fugères. But Pyat's interest in social causes and his career as a melodramatist were of longer standing. He had come to Paris a young firebrand liberal, had seen his first play produced when he was only twenty-two (1832) and had gone on to become a regular member of Parisian literary circles. He collaborated with other playwrights, got to know Jules Sandeau and knew George Sand before she took that name. He was a charter member of Balzac's Society of Men of Letters (writers trying, in the absence of copyright laws, to protect themselves against literary piracy). He had little trouble in making a name for himself as an obstreperous political radical and as a writer of abrasively interesting dramas. Bombast and contrivings were his theatrical stock in trade, but he offered a melodrama that was thoroughly contemporary. This explains its great success.

His play opened with heavy theatricality to show a miserable slum attic, "without furniture, without fire, almost without light."[22] Through broken panes of the window wind and rain poured in. Stage left in this dreary room sat a dying old man, his legs wrapped in a tattered blanket. Stage right, in a battered crib lay a tiny child. Between them, center stage, stood Paul Davis who delivered himself of the opening lines. "My father, my poor father, how are you feeling this morning? You had a bad night . . . you are still suffering greatly, I see it, I feel it. . . ." The oldster replied, "Thank you, Paul, thank you . . . you have watched over me night

"I've come for the rent."

and day, my good Paul, without thinking that you owed your labors to your child."[23] The audience soon learned how the old laborer, upright and honest his whole life long, had come upon such hard times, how his two motherless sons, Paul and George, had become skilled locksmiths but, out of work, could no longer acquit themselves honorably of their debts. Now, not a cent could be found to pay a doctor, for medicine, food for the tiny child or even the rent (yes, the landlord did come for the rent!).

Then the scene shifted to the opulent home of Murray, the evil banker. This heartless financier had lost the key to his strongbox and was obliged to call urgently upon Paul, who had made the lock, to furnish him with another key. By happy chance, Murray's lovely daughter, Jenny, was present when Paul arrived to pen the safe. Loving, generous, wide-eyed and compassionate, she felt stirrings of a strange attraction for this skillful, sturdy, virtuous worker. . . .

As the play ended, Paul, now found to be of noble family, and his true love Jenny stood together at center stage to consider the beatitude of marriage and of living together "rich and happy." Meanwhile the audience had been given a wrenching picture of the exact circumstances of poverty, of the pitiful and shameful alternatives the poor were obliged to choose from. Melodramatic, contemporary and trenchant, *The Two Locksmiths* succeeded enormously where *The Burgraves* had failed. Clearly the situations and social problems that now preoccupied the popular novelists and melodramatists were the same ones that increasingly claimed the attention of the public at large. These things were in the air. The expression and illustration they received in the popular literature were crude, but the problems themselves were far more than simply literary fashions. They were concerns that affected the entire nation, rents in the social fabric of France.

In 1846 Pyat presented another of his excess-ridden dramas, *Diogène*. Again the thrust of his work was the outrage, the cruelty and the injustice the rich work upon the virtuous poor. Again the play caused a great *succès de scandale*. Pyat needed little encouragement to go right back to work; like Oscar Wilde, he too was discovering that nothing succeeded like excess. The next year his final, most overblown creation appeared on stage. *The Ragpicker of Paris* opened in a theater that had always specialized in melodramas, the Porte St.-Martin, in May of 1847. The audience was given a tour of the seamiest sides of Parisian slums through five acts of frenzied exaggeration which included twelve tableaux and a prologue in which only the first of several on-stage murders was committed. Little was spared the viewer: murders, children bought, sold or left for death, procuresses and shadowy plots. All this came to the eyes or passed through the hands of the ragpicker whose pointed stick and burlap bag collected the debris of Paris. This was the most virulent attack, contained the most vitriolic apostrophizing Pyat was capable of. There were plenty of chances here for Pyat to have his trashpile Diogenes comment acidly upon actuality, philosophize sadly and speculate in yearning. Frédérick LeMaître who played the role stopped the show and brought down the house when, sifting through his day's scavengings, he pulled from his sack an old crown and remarked that

this "had served." The crowd easily understood:
monarchy had seen its day and should now be thrown
away.

CHAPTER VII

Last Days of the Popular Literature

➤➤ *LIKE SOME RANK WEED, THE POPULAR LITERATURE GREW,* flourished and rapidly died. But while still in its full maturity it came to vigorous seed. Its progeny accomplished a most potent and important cultural cross-breeding.

In 1848 the melodrama had only recently burst out of the rude booths of the seasonal fairs, and the cheap novel had had an exceedingly short time of telling wildly implausible stories in impossibly vulgar fashion. Curiously, one branch of the popular literature nurtured the other, allowing both to grow still stronger. The melodrama fed upon the novel for its stories; Ducray-Duminil wrote his cheap imitations of the English Gothic novel and Pixérécourt, snipping and pasting, promptly used them to throw together dramas designed to wring tears from credulous Parisian concierges.

Yet despite their flaws, both genres found their ill-educated audience, increased mightily in their favor and, finally, ended by constituting a presence upon the literary scene which would not simply go away. In the lending libraries, the popular novels outrented all others. On Paris's Boulevard du Crime, cheap theaters packed their houses by offering an exclusive diet of melodrama, act one devoted to virtue, act two to suffering and act three to the triumph of love.

Understandably, well-bred literature ignored this upstart form, thankful for the distinctions that separated them. Respectable Parisian theaters maintained their virtue. They huddled about a noble if outworn tradition, while outside, in the cultural slums, an ignorant mass wallowed in the purgation of melodrama.

But inevitably this situation changed. Class distinctions between the two literatures began to erode, to fade away. It was speeded along by the most powerful of solvents, money. It happened first in the drama.

Young Romantics, literary revolutionaries in search of a battle, wanted a theater that would be different, shocking to their elders and profitable. The melodrama was all of these things, so Romantic dramatists began their literary revolt by embracing the popular drama. The opening battle was the *succès de scandale* of Hugo's *Hernani*. Important as a reference date in the struggle of Romanticism, February 25, 1930, is even more important as a date in the struggle of the popular drama. For *Hernani* was melodrama, and no mistake about it. In truth, almost all of the Romantic dramas to follow were little more than melodrama (sometimes a bit better written) with an added historical flourish. Other battles and other successes followed too. Was Soulié right to credit himself with having first forced the doors of the Comédie Française with his *Clotilde* in 1832? It matters less whose play accomplished the feat than what was accomplished. When, under the press of literary fashion, the Comédie opened its stage to Romanticism, the last, most proud redoubt of French Classicism surrendered to the strength and popularity of this "people's drama." Melodrama had won its cultural citizenship, even if it had begun with a desire to turn a profit.

The novel had to wait a bit longer for respectability but when it achieved it the motive was again economic. The theater agreed in the 1830's to treat its cloddish but muscular country cousin with respect, but the novel tarried until the early years of the next decade. In doing so, it brought upon itself even greater discomfiture. While the well-bred novel was never obliged to admit its uncouth counterpart into the intimacy of its commodious octavo format, it was forced, and for reasons directly financial, to leave its prestigious hardbound covers and follow the popular novel into the columns of the daily press, into the feuilleton. There authors fervently hoped to lessen the sting of embarrassment with the soothing urguents of success and wealth. Printing prices had risen, money was scarce and books were not selling well at all. At the same moment, though, newspapers were cheap, more people than ever were reading them, and the feuilletons were just beginning their soaring popularity.

The French novel and drama had travelled a long road between 1815 and 1848. Both had undergone major unexpected modifications. For the novel, the period had begun with the vapid novel of manners in which noble men and ladies described the plight of their tormented souls, caught up as they were in the throes of a well-bred fatal passion. Abruptly, within a few years, came Stendhal's mordant etchings of Parisian salons with an impotent hero. Soon he drew his corrosive picture of an entire French oligarchy closing ranks to execute a French peasant youth. Then followed Balzac's pedestrian heroes, retired spaghetti manufacturers, impoverished but ambitious medical students. Alternating with these were George Sand's gently poetic novels where the well polished virtues of humble souls and country bumpkins shone almost unbelievably. In contrast to these, the gargantuan evils of Sue's Parisian underworld loomed incredibly large. And, in the offing, only seven or so years later waited Flaubert's bitter and prophylactic dissection of provincial petite bourgeoisie.

So the content of the novel had changed enormously. Its setting was now contemporary, its characters, taken from real life, were beset by quite genuine problems and their social class was no longer exclusively the nobility and the genteel. Bourgeois and lower-class authors now wrote from life, of what they knew. This change in the novel, this enlarging of its scope, with its emphasis upon depicting actual conditions of living humans seems almost to foretell the coming, in another field, of the invention of the camera. More than ever before, the novel pictured human beings *pris sur le vif.* The novel was rejoining life, was becoming realistic.

In the drama the change was scarcely less startling. Until the coming of the Romantics there was precious little to replace Voltaire's disciple, Raynouard, with his plays cookie-cut from the dough of a pseudo-classical tradition. Their amalgam of melodrama and rimed historical romance pleased audiences for barely more than thirteen

years.   And when Romantic drama failed, only the
tinsel and backdrops of an historical picturesqueness
were stripped away.   All of the melodrama continued
with no more than a change in the time of the action.
Contemporary melodrama continued to please.   Pyat's
Ragpicker of Paris (1841) succeeded wildly where
Hugo's *Burgraves* (1843) failed.   Already upon the horizon were Dumas fils and Augier with their plays of
social concern.

Again the change was enormous.   Like the novel,
the drama now treated contemporary French society,
genuine people and immediate problems, the very real
iniquities of poverty and sickness.   No more could serious
dramatists move their audiences with pictures of the ills
of princesses long since dead.   Rather, dramatists portrayed the social ills of a society where a landed nobility
gave way definitively to an aristocracy based upon
money but, lamentably, in which, for the lower classes,
feudal serfdom changed only to become economic
slavery.   Playwrights pictured these changes and pleaded
for alleviations to the sufferings they brought.   The
drama too was rejoining life.   The socially concerned
thesis play was being born.

To trace the transformation of well-bred literature
in response to the popular is to demonstrate the impact
and the extent of influence of this new literature.   But
it does not explain it.   The reasons for the impact and
for the definitive modifications it brought are inter-
related but they may be grouped conveniently and accurately within the meaning of the word contemporaneity.   And the motive was money.

Seen from this vantage point, the influence of the

popular literature gains its true perspective. In 1815 literature had almost forgotten its roots in life in order to follow an abstract ideal. It had become a literature almost purely of the mind, immune to everyday living, to economic change, old age and fears. Now it discovered that it did indeed have roots which badly needed care. Empty theaters and unsold octavo volumes aptly symbolized that it had lost touch with life. The popular literature developed among the lower classes who gave it its first audience: readers of novels for chambermaids and red-faced snifflers at melodramas. This people's literature won its own huge success and, as it did so, enticed the respectable into imitating its methods and its subjects. Theaters opened their stages to melodramas and serious novelists followed the popular writers into the feuilletons. In following and in adopting a proven, lower-class formula for success there took place between the two literatures a surprising but perfectly natural phenomenon: the two melded together.

In the melding, the limits of literature were greatly enlarged, the boundaries of what it might treat and the fashions in which it could do so were vastly increased. Serious playwrights could now treat every subject available to melodramatists while sober novelists could follow the paths that the popular novel had traced. Perhaps the most striking example of this new freedom within the newly enlarged realm of literature is Victor Hugo.

Spurred by the feuilleton, Hugo incorporated in his *Les Misérables* both the techniques of the popular press and the high seriousness of the educated novel. Without the conjoining of the literatures, this feat would have been unthinkable. He used Soulié's trick of interrupting the action just when the reader wished to know more, pictured lower-class and criminal lives that Sue had made so popular and echoed the social concern that both Sue and George Sand had repeatedly shown in their feuilletons. In his novel, just as in his drama, Hugo made free and heavy use of techniques and subjects which others had pioneered. Yet, *Les Misérables* is not simply a popular novel; it is a work which could only have been written after the merging of the two literatures. It required the freedom that only the new literary realm could provide. Its author, clearly, was of the educated realm but its subject, its construction, its techniques were of the popular realm, just as was its obvious humanitarianism.

Sand, Sue and Hugo, all came separately to their genuine involvement with social concern. The reason these quite different writers came to their awareness of social ills when they did is simply that, increasingly, these ills were exacerbated by industrialization and as they became more apparent men gave more and more of their attention to them. These problems and possible solutions for them were in the air.

The 1840's were years of education for the bourgeois and the upper classes. Their interest and concern were heightened by the publication of such works as *Laboring Classes and Dangerous Classes of Paris.* The theater and feuilleton provided abundant illustrations. Accordingly, there came as well a spate of proposals to solve the problems or at least to alleviate the hurt. The St. Simoniens, the Fourierists, and the followers of the socialist, Louis Blanc, all clamored for public attention. The same situation also gave much cause for reflection to a bespectacled German economist resident in Paris during these same years. It was not mere chance that Karl Marx's *Communist Manifesto* appeared in 1848.

Nor was it providential that the melding of the two literatures into one and the recently achieved cheap daily press's feuilleton occurred just in time to publicize the wounds inflicted by France's headlong industrialization. The same rapid changes in life patterns introduced into France by the factory system multiplied the degree of social injustices and social distinctions. It also created the conditions necessary for the existence of such a press.

The rush into the cities of newly literate peasants to man the factories created the audiences for the popular literature. The economic conditions that prompted the lower price of newspapers brought the popular press within reach of this hugely increased audience. Without these rapid changes the social and political awareness, not only of the ruling classes but, more important, of the working classes, might have been long delayed.

But under the battering of novels and plays produced by the newly merged literatures, a social awareness of large proportions was forged. The bourgeois became uncomfortably aware of the horrid details of poverty, unemployment, illness and inhuman working conditions. Collectively, workers too became conscious of the enormity of these ills, of the injustice, and realized that they shared these things with a majority of their fellow countrymen. So it was that this new literature, socially concerned and democratic in thrust, played the preeminent role in politicizing the laboring classes. Without writers to give them knowledge of the problems, without drama to picture the extent and meaning of their suffering and without novels to offer hope of amelioration, partial solutions and even complete utopias, workers would doubtless not have taken the course they did.

The effect of this forging, however, was stunning. It accomplished among the laboring classes of Paris something against which not even the memories of the Revolution of 1830, and "days" of 1832 and 1835 could prevail. During all of these uprisings the laborers had been the cat's paw for the bourgeoisie; they had rebelled, had overthrown the government in bloody fighting only to see the bourgeoisie scoop up the prizes and the power. But this time so strong was their certitude that their pleas had been heard that they took to the streets once more. They forgot that they had been used, time and again, cynically and ruthlessly. The working classes of Paris entered into still another uneasy alliance with the bourgeois. They joined forces with their employers, their masters in rejection of Louis Philippe's government.

It seemed at first to be just another Paris street rebellion. Troops were called out to quell minor riots over the government's forbidding of an anti-government banquet and speech-making occasion. As before, rather than dispersing the crowds, the troops fired shots into them and killed some fifty citizens at the massacre of the Boulevard des Capucines. The people rose up in earnest, the King abdicated, and even as the interim government tried to get itself organized, Louis Philippe left Paris in the most bourgeois of fashions, by taxi.

While the leaders of state gathered, undecided as to whether to declare for another monarchy, a regency, an empire or another republic, the people moved decisively to force the republic. The waves of sentimental socialism which the new literature had energetically stirred now came to lap at the very feet of the men who were trying to form a government. Workers arrived at the Hôtel de Ville to give voice to their expectations, petitions, and demands. Delegations from a variety of political groups harangued the beleaguered politicians. Reform had been the general cry of the political opposition before the uprising but now the word was used with a much more radical connotation, at least in the minds of the workers. Bourgeois users of the word envisioned little more than a cautious enlarging of the electoral base, a gentle and purely political reform. The workers, they soon discovered, had understood much more by "reform." For them it meant social reform and on a nationwide scale. All the hopes raised among them by all the novels and plays which glorified the workers and mocked the pear shape of the well-fed bourgeois now came together in a swell of aggressive enthusiasm, of hopes that would not be denied.

As the speeches went on and as the men in the Hôtel took measure of the crowd's expectations, bourgeois hopes for a nicely limited revolt gave way to grudging acceptance of popular demands. The Second Republic would function with universal suffrage. Officials listened with grave attention to a young man armed with a rifle who demanded that the government recognize the right of every man to work, that government organize labor so as to assure a minimum pay for the worker and his family. In reply, the state pledged to guarantee the existence of the workers by providing

work. The next day it decreed the creation of National Workshops to give the unemployed jobs. On February 28th, it was impressed enough by an angry workers' demonstration to authorize a Commission of Labor and to recommend further labor legislation. It even seemed to be moving toward free education, toward the modernization of agriculture, industry and commerce. Albert, a semi-literate worker, was named to serve in the new government to represent the laborers. In almost every field the workers were winning impressive concessions. They nearly changed the flag of France. They shouted for the red banner of radical social revolution and very nearly carried the day. It took Lamartine, the tireless talker, to talk them out of it. "The red flag has merely made the circuit of the Champ de Mars, dragged in the people's blood [while] the tricolor flag has gone round the world with the name, the glory and the freedom of the Fatherland."[1]

So much of what was enacted into law by the new government only echoed earlier demands and earlier solutions offered by the popular literature, particularly the novels of Sue, that it was very nearly as if the new rulers were following the novelist's program. There was, from *Mysteries,* the abolition of the death penalty in matters political, and the organization of labor. From *The Jew*, the creation of national workshops and distribution of food to the poor, and from *Martin,* free medical care. More, there was the abolition of slavery in the colonies, the end of the Black Code, abolition of titles of nobility, an end to imprisonment for debt and corporal punishment. Under pressure, the bourgeois and workers were reaching agreement and accommodation. Society was beginning to jell.

Powerfully at work in this partial political unification was an earlier memory, now almost a dream, of liberty, equality and fraternity. To this both groups could respond emotionally if not ideologically. Emotion led their minds to link the settling of contemporary political and social problems with an older dream. Both well-bred and popular literature urged humanitarian ideals of justice, pictured as very real and quite near men's dreams of a world of peace and concord. The message of the popular literature had penetrated deeply into the respectable literature. Facing new challenges, the government claimed its legitimacy from the first revolutionary republic. But with good bourgeois caution the governmental leaders took care, in proclaiming the Second Republic, to assure that there would be no renewal of the "terror" associated with the first.

The Revolution of 1848 was the revolution of the feuilleton and of the melodrama, in short, of the popular literature. It was the feuilleton which initiated the great Parisian masses into seeing their desperate situation as political and social problems. It created and whetted the appetite of the Parisian workers for workable solutions, both political and social. The democratic society of the Second Republic was born of the democratic literature. Sadly, the Second Republic would falter and fall precisely because it had read too many novels, seen too many plays and had been lulled by its hopes into a dream whose time clearly had not yet come. Yet, for the moment, the victory was terribly sweet.

The leader of the victorious feuilletonists was Eugène Sue, the dandy turned socialist. Of course he would enter political life. Prophetically, in the mardi gras parade of 1846 Sue had already been hailed as a conquering warrior. The publisher Joly had arranged a gaudily impressive allegorical float to travel the streets of Paris in honor of the feuilletons. Standing upon it were four paladins bearing banners which carried the names of the champions of the feuilletons: Soulié, Sand, Sue and Dumas. Soulié had died in 1847, and Dumas was not much interested in politics. His literary factory's production specialized in historical romances. But Sue and Sand were feverishly interested and passionately involved, as was Félix Pyat.

When dates for elections were set, all three entered into active preparations. Sue stood for office from Le Loiret and put his pen to declarations of socialist plans and principles. "Mindful of having for a long time and to the limit of my strengths served the cause, [I] offer my past as guarantee of the future . . . adherence heart and soul to the form and spirit of republican government, the firm intention of demanding with all its political and social consequences the application of this immortal principle: liberty, equality and fraternity."[2]

Sand with her typical wholehearted impetuousness rushed back and forth between Paris and Berry where she hoped to lead the peasants into the bright new world of light. Pyat was sent by the new government as commissioner to Le Cher where he explained tirelessly to the peasantry the glories of the new republic. Even Dumas and Hugo, a peer of the former realm, decided to stand for office as deputies.

But in the first elections, only Pyat was sent to

Paris a winner in the contests. Voters in the rest of the
areas were still intensely conservative, still looked to the
village priest for guidance in matters political. Moreover, they mistrusted many of the representatives that
Paris had sent out to help them. The Revolution had
taken place in Paris, not in the provinces. If electors
did not reject the Revolution, they nonetheless sent to
the capital to speak for them men whom they did not
suspect of being tainted with radicalism. Neither Sue
nor Sand nor Hugo nor Dumas inspired confidence in
the voters but, significantly, a certain Louis-Napoleon
Bonaparte was elected from several departments.

A renewed effort by Sue in runoff elections finally
did bring him to the Chamber. Voted against by
the richer quarters of Paris and by the still conservative semi-rural areas, he was elected by the solid
voting of the poor sections of Paris. Here lived the avid
readers of the feuilletons, the petty bourgeois and the
workers.

Sue's career in politics symbolizes in some sort the
brief life of the Second Republic, that uneasy alliance
between the people and the bourgeois. Having won
election to the Chamber, Sue prescinded from exercising
his rights as a deputy. Rather than function as a representative of the people he championed so ardently, he
literally spent his time there correcting proofs of his
serials. He simply was not a political animal. His
socialism was of the theoretical, sentimental, humanitarian sort; he was totally unfit and even uninterested in
fighting the parliamentary struggles required to translate
dreamy ideals into practical programs. So it was that
Sue, brought to office by universal suffrage, looked on

while the assembly decided to do away with the slow but sure poison of the vote. In May of 1850 the Chamber stripped three million Frenchmen of their voting rights. The bourgeois was changing its mind, was drawing away from its alliance.

In so doing, the bourgeois moved with a precision that was both direct and symbolic. The feuilleton had brought Sue the people's representative, into the government. Now the government moved to punishment. The Chamber voted the Riancy law (1850) obliging newspapers and purchasers to pay a special tax of five sous per copy of any journal containing a "novelistic work." This step effectively precluded any possibility of social reformers wrapping their proposals attractively in the bright popularity of the continued serial. Under the threat of this discriminatory and prohibitive tax, newspapers replaced the serialized novel with travel literature and other bland untaxable fare. The feuilleton was forced out of existence.

The government knew precisely why this step was required; it knew who its enemy was and who its leader. In 1851 the Academy of Châlons-sur-Marne sponsored an essay contest and chose as the topic, "The Influence of French Literature From 1830 to 1850 Upon the Public Mind and Manners." The laureate of the group (*and* Secretary General of the police of Lyons) minced no words. Popular literature was the enemy and Sue was its leader. "For twenty years," he thundered, "in all his novels Sue has, by degrees, innoculated the people with his ideas, his calumnies, his excitations, his appeals to revolt and to war. When . . . in 1848, society had to defend itself against the most formidable of insurrections

. . . what were these wretches [the people] saying? They were saying and they were thinking what Sue had said and thought. They put his novels into action . . . they came up, weapons in their hands, to claim their share of rights and happiness."[3] The feuilleton serial had been too successful, too powerfully influential; its very success had brought about these attacks.

Few seemed to mourn the passing of the feuilleton. Literary tastes had changed among the bourgeois. The Revolution and the ominous specters of genuine social change had seen to that. Literature, like politics, changed régime hastily. With Napoleon's 1851 coup d'état the short lived Second Republic gave way to the stolid stability of the Second Empire. Readers wanted no more dreams, literary or political, and no more dreaming novelists.

Criticism rather than creativity seemed to suit the mood of the reading public. Critics like Sainte Beuve hastened to fill the columns vacated by the vanished serials. As the serials disappeared he accepted an offer from Véron of the Constitutionnel to write weekly articles of literary criticism. Sainte Beuve had never liked the industrialized literature nor its democratic thrust. He poured into his judgments both the contempt of his acutely sensitive mind and the vengeful urgings of his unhappy nature. In his columns he called Hugo a "cyclopean," Balzac an "Asiatic." At Balzac's death from overwork in forcing success from his serial novels, Sainte Beuve, while denying any personal bias, could find nothing more to say of his work than that it was "one of the most curious paintings of the mores of the time."[4]

Balzac was dead, Soulié had died in 1847, Sand forgot her socializing novels and returned to poeticizing country life. Sue continued to write his mammoth *Seven Capital Sins* but to an ever decreasing audience. The serials were gone and with them his public. Soon, in 1857, the public would read Flaubert's disabused tale of a woman led astray by too much reading of impossible romantic tales. France was in a clinical mood. The final form of the popular novel of the Restoration, the feuilleton was dead. It had succumbed to a surfeit of popularity.

Yet, this people's literature had exercised an extraordinary and decisive influence in the newly enlarged realm of literature and upon the whole of French sociopolitical life.

Begun as a diversion for the uneducated and easily amused, crass in motive, clumsy in construction and ignoble in subject matter, the cheap novels and the ridiculous melodramas had grown to wield a compelling power over the well bred. The realism and penchant for strongly dramatic effects were now accepted, even required aspects of all French literature. Or, to put the matter in other terms, until the coming of the popular, the respectable literature badly lacked relevance. By embracing wholeheartedly the manner and matter of the common genres, it renewed itself from the common soil, and having done so acquired an importance and a prestige essential to its own survival.

There is little if any exaggeration in asserting that French realism and naturalism stem directly from this literature created for the pleasure (and tears) of chambermaids. The links that join Restif's vignettes of attractively helpless pea shellers to Balzac's pasta manufacturer and to Flaubert's pharmacist, Homais, are unmistakable. That consummate artist, Flaubert, could not have found his realism nor his subject matter had he not been the inheritor of the work of these literary forebears. Indignant he might be, out of snobbishness, but deny he could not that in his *Bovary,* his *Simple Heart,* and his *Bouvard and Pécuchet* the genes of the popular literature run true to kind and strong. Nor does the literary historian have the slightest trouble in discerning upon the horizon another literary figure in which the same family traits predominate. Zola's generous indignation over the sorry lot of the laboring classes, his precision in detailing their fear-filled and tortured lives, his melodramatics in bringing to a bourgeois audience the shameful tale of poverty, disease, despair and vice; these too owe their very existence to the literary inheritance he assumed and built upon. Not only did the popular literature gain social entrée, it also changed definitively the direction French literature was to take.

Paralleling the struggle for admission of the little regarded genres into social respectability was the struggle of the French people themselves to gain entrée into the life of their own nation. Just as the popular literature had fought its fights and forced the austere battlements of the well-bred literature, so the people waged their own tenacious struggle for recognition. Uncounted, non voting, unconsulted in decision making, their efforts for reform, to participate in the life of France make this century of French history the tale of a country on the path towards a liberal democratic society. In this struggle too the popular literature in concert with the re-

spectable worked powerfully and with finality. The
role of writers was of great importance. It was they who
prepared the ground, who raised questions and hopes
among the poor, who created a level of expectation
among the laboring classes so that they eagerly gathered
in the streets once again, to throw up their barricades
and to rebel that unexpected day of February 25, 1848.

In acceding to the shouts and demands of the
workers, the creators of the Second Republic were,
without knowing it, doing rather more than simply em-
ploying canny tactics. They were not merely giving
ground one day to regain it the next. In truth, the social
and political oligarchy was being hammered into a quite
different shape. France in 1848 was still far from its
egalitarian ideal; it was still to see another Empire and
another military defeat before it could try a third time
for a Republic.

Nonetheless, France had undergone fundamental
changes: the political oligarchy had been breached as
had the literary oligarchy. The requirements of the
people, if not welcomed, were at least acknowledged.
Henceforth, their rulers would give them wary and ap-
praising attention. Wisely, Louis-Napoleon chose to
submit his coup d'état to the people for ratification in
universal suffrage. Now the political importance of the
masses could only grow.

The importance of this breaching was precisely that
it was unlike other earlier riots and changes of régime.
This was not to prove merely another preempting by
the upper classes of gains won by the lower. This was
no rough peasant dance, more energetic than decorous,
which the nobility could take up, smooth and polish to

make of it an amusement for the genteel, where fine ladies might bow and twirl with studied grace. While Emma Bovary spun and swooned at the noble ball at Vaubyessard, servants and peasants stared in through the windows at her in curiosity and envy. But they could not be kept forever from joining the dance. Soon they would consider shouldering their way boldly into the ballroom to take part in the fete. It was, after all, their dance; ladies and gentlemen danced to a tune they had written. Just as their literature had radically transformed the reading of the gentry, so their political and social presence would now begin slowly to transform the internal politics of the nation.

In French literature and in French life, the popular literature had sown fateful seeds. Short lived itself, it contributed predominantly to revivifying, enlarging and freeing that literature. It was able now to treat any and all levels of society. That this literature then became humanitarian and democratic was again due to the dominant influence of the people's literature.

Few would seek to argue that the course of literature and that of democracy are necessarily intertwined. It is not so: literature, can apparently, flourish under all manner of kings and emperors. But such was indeed the case during the first half of the last century in France. Literature and democracy did meet and conjoin. The development of a popular literature and of a powerful and growing impetus towards a liberal democratic society were parallel and mutually supportive phenomena.

For long France has determinedly cultivated the arts of literature and of government. Seldom have the two combined more happily to raise men's hopes than at that time. Believers in democracy who study its uneven growth in that country will find much in her fiction to read and to reflect upon. Similarly, students of fiction who trace the literary history of the period will find much of her social and political life laid before their eyes. Thoughtful men, enamored of both, cannot fail to find in the study of those years an abundance of artifacts that must prove of deepest interest and instruction to them.

Indeed, the temptation is great for eager ideals to declare what logic dares not: that democracy and literature should by rights stride forward together toward the betterment of man. Yet, if one must reluctantly draw back from such a declaration, it is still possible to affirm that in this instance the one did indeed fertilize and succor the other. One is obliged also to affirm that, for this period of time and in this country, neither one can be studied or truly understood without the other.

CHAPTER NOTES

CHAPTER I

[1]"Lettres inédites d'Alfred de Vigny à Victor Hugo," *Revue des Deux Mondes*, 1 fév. 1925, p. 516.

CHAPTER II

[1]Ad. Paupe and P. A. Chéramy, *Correspondance de Stendhal, 1800-1842*, Paris, Eds. le Divan, 1888, Vol. III, pp. 88-92.

[2]*Les Misérables*, N. Y., Thomas Y. Crowell, 1887, Part IV, Bk. 7., p. 165.

[3]*Gustave ou le mauvais sujet*, Paris, Jules Rouff, s.d., p. 81.

[4]Alice M. Killen, *Le Roman "terrifiant" ou roman "noir" de Walpole à Anne Radcliffe et son influence sur la littérature française jusqu'en 1840*, Paris, Georges Crès et cie, 1915, p. 131.

[5]*Courrier anglais* (Letter of Sept. 21, 1828), Paris, le Divan, 1935, Vol. III, p. 432.

[6]Eric Partridge, *The French Romantic's Knowledge of English Literature (1820-1848) According to Contemporary French Memoirs, Letters and Periodicals*, Vol. XIV of *Bibliographie de la revue de la littérature comparée*, Paris, Champion,

1924, p. 210.

[7] *Coelina*, Paris, 1803, p. 42.

[8] *Ibid.*, p. 54.

[9] *Journal des Petites Affiches*, 19 Fructidor, an VIII.

[10] *La Femme à deux maris*, Paris, 1802, p. 71.

[11] *Christophe Colomb*, Paris, Barba, 1815, pp. 67-68.

[12] *Ibid.*

[13] *Le Globe*, 23 juin 1827.   [14] *Ibid.*

[15] 4 nov. 1833.

[16] Paul Ginisty, *Le Mélodrame*, Paris, Louis Michand, 1910, p. 95.

CHAPTER III

[1] Paupe and Chéramy, *Courrier anglais*, Paris, le Divan, 1935-36, Vol. III, p. 366.

[2] Paris, Barba, 1820, Vol. III, pp. 218-220.

[3] Vol. II, p. 110-111.

[4] *Valentine*, Paris, Barba, 1820, Vol. II, p. 34.

[5] Lucas-Dubreton, *La Restauration et la monarchie de juillet*, Paris, Funck-Brentano, 1926, p. 89.

[6] *Thélène*, Paris, Pollet, 1823, Vol. II, p. 202.

CHAPTER IV

[1] Maurice Bardèche, *Balzac romancier, la formation de l'art du roman chez Balzac jusqu'à la publication du "Père Goriot" 1822-1835*, Paris, Plon, 1940, p. 119.

[2] *Ibid.*, p. 92.

CHAPTER V

[1] Nora Atkinson, *Eugène Sue et le roman feuilleton*, Nemours, Lesot, doctoral thesis, 1929, p. 10.

[2] *Ibid.*

[3] Jean-Louis Bory, *Eugène Sue — le roi du roman populaire*, Paris, Hachette, 1962, pp. 272-273.

[4]Atkinson, *op. cit.*, p. 12.

[5]L. Reybaud, *Jérôme Paturot à la recherche d'une position sociale,* Paris, Club Français du Livre, 1965, pp. 66-67.

[6]*Les Deux Cadavres,* Paris, Michel Lévy, 1870, p. 312.

[7]G.W.M. Reynolds, *The Modern Literature of France,* London, 1839, I, p. 113.

[8]*Théâtre de Frédéric Soulié 1840-42,* Paris, Souverain, /Preface to Vol. I, p. 71.

[9]Quoted in Harold March, *Frédéric Soulié Novelist and Dramatist of the Romantic Period,* New Haven, Yale, 1931, p. 172.

[10]*Les Mémoires du diable,* Paris, Ambroise Dupont, 1837-38, Vol. I, p. 5.

[11]*Ibid.,* pp. 14-15.

CHAPTER VI

[1]Eugène Sue, *The Salamander,* translated by H. W. Herbert, New York, Winchester, 1844, preface, p. xi.

[2]Jean-Louis Bory, *Eugène Sue le roi du roman populaire,* Paris, Hachette, 1962, pp. 171-172.

[3]Paris, Paulin, 1845, pp. 235-236.

[4]"Souvenirs littéraires," *Revue de Paris et de Saint Pétersbourg,* fév. 1888. Vol. II, p. 19.

[5]Bory, p. 243.

[6]*Journal des Débats,* 8 fév. 1843, p. 1. (Deleted in subsequent editions of the *Mysteries.*)

[7]Bory, p. 271.   [8]*Ibid.,* p. 279.

[9]*Ibid.,* p. 284.   [10]*Ibid.,* p. 279.

[11]*Ibid.,* p. 286.

[12]*Le Juif errant,* Brussels, Méline, Cans et Cie, 1846, Vol. I, pp. 1-2.

[13]*Chroniques Parisiennes 1843-1845,* 11 août 1845, Paris, Calmann Lévy, 1876.

[14]"Lettres critiques sur *Le Juif errant* de Sue," *La Gazette de France,* 8 nov. 1844.

[15]"Lettres à Madame Hanska," *Oeuvres complètes,* XXVI,

Paris, Les Bibliophiles de l'Originale, Vol. II of letters, 1968 (letter of Sept. 11, 1844), p. 535.

[16] *Ibid.*

[17] Letter to Laprade, quoted in Wladimir Karénine, *George Sand, sa vie et ses oeuvres,* Paris, Plon, 1912, Vol. III, p. 504.

[18] *Lettres à l'étrangère,* Paris, Calmann Lévy, 1950 (letter of 11 nov. 1846), Vol. IV, p. 114.

[19] *Les Trois mousquetaires,* Paris, Calmann Lévy, s.d., pp. 130-131.

[20] Paris, Pléiade, 1964, Vol. II, p. 25.

[21] *Ibid.,* p. 26.

[22] *Les Deux serruriers,* Paris, Au Répertoire Dramatique, 1841, Scene I, Act I (pages unnumbered).

[23] *Ibid.*

CHAPTER VII

[1] André Maurois, *The Miracle of France,* New York, Harper, 1958, pp. 342-343.

[2] Bory, *op, cit.,* p. 327.   [3] *Ibid.,* p. 350.

[4] *Le Constitutionnel,* Sept. 2, 1850.

BIBLIOGRAPHY

I. The Novel

Ducange, Victor, *Oeuvres complètes*, Paris, Lecointe et Pougin, 1833-1838, a reprinting of the following novels:

Agathe, ou le petit vieillard de Calais (1819)
Albert, ou les amants missionnaires (1820)
Valentine, ou le pasteur d'Uzès (1820)
Thélène, ou l'amour et la guerre (1823)
Léonide, ou la vieille de Surènes (1823)
Le Médecin confesseur, ou la jeune émigrée (1825)
La Luthérienne, ou la famille morave (1825)
Les Trois filles de la veuve (1826)
Isaurine et Jean-Pohl, ou les révolutions du château de Gît-au-Diable (1827)
Ludovica ou le testament de Waterloo (1830)
Marc-Loricot, ou le petit chouan de 1830 (1830)

Les Moeurs, contes et nouvelles (posthumous, 1834)

Joasine, ou la fille du prêtre (posthumous, 1835)

Ducray-Duminil, François Guillaume, *Victor ou l'enfant de la forêt,* Paris, Belin-Le Prieur, 1814.

Hugo, Victor, *Les Misérables,* N. Y., Thomas Y. Crowell, 1887.

Kock, Paul de, *Gustave ou le mauvais sujet,* Paris, Jules Rouff, s.d.

Pigault-Lebrun, Charles Antoine Guillaume, *Oeuvres complètes,* Paris, Barba, 1822-1829.

Restif de la Bretonne, *Les Contemporaines,* Paris, Marpon et Flammarion, 1875-1876.

Sand, George, *Oeuvres complètes,* Paris, Calmann Lévy, 1925.

Soulié, Frédéric, *Confession générale,* Paris, Souverain, 1840-1847.

   Les Deux Cadavres, Paris, Michel Lévy, 1870.

   Marguerite, Paris, Souverain, 1842.

   Les Mémoires du diable, Paris, Ambroise Dupont, 1837-1838.

Stendhal (Henri Beyle), *Oeuvres complètes,* Paris, le Divan, s.d.

Sue, Eugène, *Oeuvres,* Paris, C. Marpon et E. Flammarion s.d.

   Le Juif errant, Brussels, Méline, et Cans et Cie, 1848.

   The Salamander, translated by H. W. Herbert, N. Y., Winchester, 1844.

II. Theatre

Caigniez, Louis Charles, *La Pie voleuse ou la servante de Palaiseau*, Paris, Barba, 1815.

Ducange, Victor, *Le Jésuite*, Paris, Tresse, 1840.

>*Trente ans, ou la vie d'un joueur*, Paris, Tresse, 1856.

Hugo, Victor, "Les Burgraves," *Théâtre*, Vol. II, Paris, Pléiade, 1964.

Pyat, Félix, *Le Brigand et le philosophe*, Paris, Duvernois, 1834.

>*Le Chiffonnier de Paris*, Paris, 1847.

>*Les Deux serruriers*, Paris, Au Répertoire Dramatique, 1841.

Pixérécourt, René Charles Guilbert de, *Théâtre choisi*, Introduction par Ch. Nodier, Paris, Tresse, 1841-1842.

>*Christophe Colomb où la découverte du nouveau monde*, Paris, Barba, 1815.

>*Coelina ou l'enfant du mystère*, Paris, 1803 (pamphlet).

>*La Femme à deux maris*, Paris, 1802.

Soulié, Frédéric, *Clotilde*, Paris, 1832.

III.   Secondary Sources

Albert, Maurice, *Littérature française sous la révolution, l'empire et la restauration*, Paris, Lecène, Oudin et Cie., 1891.

>*Les Théâtres des boulevards, 1789-1848,*

164

Paris, Société Française
d'Imprimerie et de Librairie, 1902.

Ariste, Paul de, *La Vie et le monde du boulevard, 1830-
1870,* Paris, Callandrier, 1930.

Artz, F. B., *France under the Bourbon Restoration,
1814-1830,* Cambridge, Mass., Harvard University
Press, 1931.

Atkinson, Nora, *Eugène Sue et le roman-feuilleton,*
Nemours, France, A. Lesot, 1929 (doctoral thesis).

Balzac, Honoré de, *Lettres à l'étrangère,* Vol. IV, Paris,
Calmann Lévy, 1940.

       Oeuvres complètes, Vol. XXVI, Paris, Les
       Bibliophiles de l'Originale,
       Vol. II of "Lettres à Madame
       Hanska," 1968.

Barba, J. N., *Souvenirs,* Paris, Ledoyen et Giret, 1846.

Bardèche, Maurice, *Balzac romancier, la formation de
l'art du roman chez Balzac jusqu'à la publication
du "Père Goriot" 1822-1835,* Paris, Plon, 1940.

Bégué, Armand, *Etat présent des études sur Restif de
la Bretonne,* Paris, Belles Lettres, 1948.

Beuchat, Charles, *De Restif à Flaubert ou le naturalisme
en marche,* Paris, Les Editions la Bourdonnais, s.d.

Bonnefon, Daniel, *Les Ecrivains modernes de la France
depuis le premier empire jusqu'à nos jours,* Paris,
Sandoz et Fischbacher, 1880.

Bory, Jean-Louis, *Eugène Sue — le roi du roman populaire,* Paris, Hachette, 1962.

Bosset, G. F., *F. Cooper et le roman d'aventures en
France vers 1830,* Paris, Vrin, 1928.

Brogan, D. W., *The French Nation from Napoleon to
Pétain, 1814-1940,* N. Y., Harper Colophon, 1963.

Burnand, Robert, *La Vie quotidienne en 1830, documentations de Marie-Thérèse May,* Paris, Hachette, 1957.

Champfleury, J. F., *Les Vignettes romantiques, histoire de la littérature et de l'art (1825-1840),* Paris, Dentu, 1883.

Charlety, S., *La Restauration (1815-1830),* Vol. IV of *Histoire de France contemporaine depuis la révolution jusqu'à la paix de 1919,* Paris, Hachette, 1921.

Chaunu, Pierre, *Eugène Sue et la seconde république,* Paris, Presses Universitaires de France, 1948.

Chevalier, Louis, *Classes laborieuses et classes dangereuses de Paris,* Paris, 1958.

Clouard, Henri, *Alexandre Dumas,* Paris, Eds. Albin Michel, 1955.

Cuvillier, Armand, *Hommes et idéologies de 1840,* Paris, Librairie M. Rivières, 1956.

Desgranges, Charles M., *Le Romantisme et la critique, la presse littéraire sous le restauration, 1815-1830,* Paris, Société du Mercure de France, 1907.

Dollet, R., *Stendhal journaliste,* Paris, Mercure de France, 1948.

Evans, D. O., *Le Roman moderne à l'époque romantique,* Paris, J. Budry et Cie., 1923.

  Les Problèmes d'actualité au théâtre à l'époque romantique, 1827-1850, thèse, Paris, Eds. de la Vie Universitaire, 1923.

Feletz, C.M.D., *Jugements historiques et littéraires sur quelques écrivains et quelques écritures du temps,* Paris, 1840.

Gandon, Yves, *Cent ans de jargon ou de l'écriture*

artiste au style canaille, Paris, Haumont, 1951.

Ginisty, Paul, *Le Mélodrame,* Bibliothèque Théâtrale Illustrée, Paris, Louis Michaud, 1910.

    Le Théâtre de la rue, Paris, Eds. Albert Morance, 1925.

Grant, Elliott M., *The Career of Victor Hugo,* Cambridge, Harvard University Press, 1946.

Hartog, Willie G., *Guilbert de Pixérécourt, sa vie, son mélodrame, sa technique et son influence,* Paris, H. Champion, 1913.

Johannet, R., *Evolution du roman-social,* Reims, 1908.

Jourda, Pierre, "Un Cabinet de lecture en province en 1832," *Revue d'Histoire Littéraire de la France,* Vol. XLIV.

    Etat présent des études stendhaliennes, Paris, Les Belles Lettres, 1930.

Karénine, Wladimir, *George Sand, sa vie et ses oeuvres,* Paris, Plon, 1912.

Killen, Alice M., *Le Roman "terrifiant" ou roman "noir" de Walpole à Anne Radcliffe et son influence sur la littérature française jusqu'en 1840,* Paris, Georges Crès et Cie., 1915.

Lacey, Alexander, *Pixérécourt and the French Romantic Drama,* Toronto, University of Toronto Press, 1928.

Le Breton, André, *Le Roman français au XIXe siècle avant Balzac,* Paris, Boivin et Cie., s.d.

Legouvé, Ernest, *Soixante ans de souvenirs,* Paris, 1886.

Levasseur, E., *Histoire des classes ouvrières en France depuis 1789 jusqu'à nos jours,* Vol. I, Paris, Hachette, 1867.

Louvancourt, Henri, *De Henri de Saint-Simon à Charles Fourier, étude sur le socialisme romantique français de 1830,* Paris, thesis, Faculty of Law, 1913.

Lucas-Dubreton, J., *La Restauration et la monarchie de juillet, l'histoire de France racontée à tous,* Paris, Funck-Brentano, 1926.

March, Harold, *Frédéric Soulié, Novelist and Dramatist of the Romantic Period,* New Haven, Yale University Press, 1931.

Maurois, André, *The Miracle of France,* N. Y., Harper, 1948.

"Mélodrame," *Grand dictionnaire universel du XIXe siècle,* Vol. X, E. Larousse, ed., Paris, Larousse, s.d.

Minor, Lucian W., *Victor Henri Ducange: A Participant in French Restoration Life and its Interpreter,* Unpublished Ph.D. dissertation, Boston University, 1961.

Moody, John, *Les Idées sociales d'Eugène Sue,* Paris, Presses Universitaires, 1938.

Nettement, Alfred, *Histoire de la littérature française sous la restauration,* Paris, Lecoffre, 1858.

Palache, John Garber, *Four Novelists of the Old Regime: Crébillon, Laclos, Diderot, Restif de la Bretonne,* N. Y. Viking Press, 1926.

Partridge, Eric, *The French Romantic's Knowledge of English Literature (1820-1848) according to Contemporary French Memoirs, Letters and Periodicals,* Vol. XIV of *Bibliographie de la Revue de la Littérature Comparée,* Edited by Baldensperger and Hazard, Paris, Champion, 1924.

"Paul de Kock," *Grand dictionnaire universel du XIXe siècle,* Vol. XIII, Paris, Larousse, s.d.

Reybaud, L., *Jérôme Paturot à la recherche d'une position sociale,* Paris, Classiques Français du Livre,

1965.

Reynolds, G.W.M., *The Modern Literature of France,* London, 1839.

Royer, Alphonse, *Histoire du théâtre contemporain depuis 1800 jusqu'à 1875,* Vol. V of *Histoire Universelle du Théâtre,* Paris, Paul Bellendorf, 1878.

Simon, Charles, *La Vie parisienne à travers le XIXe siècle,* Paris, 1900.

Streeter, H. W., *The Eighteenth Century English Novel in French Translation, A Bibliographical Study,* Ph.D. dissertation, Columbia University, N. Y., 1936.

Sue, Eugène, *Fonds. Bibliographie historique de la ville de Paris.*

Switzer, Parry R., *Etienne Léon de Lamothe-Langon and the French Popular Novel, 1800-1830,* Unpublished Ph.D. dissertation, University of California, Berkeley, 1955.

Thibert, Marguerite, *Le Rôle social de l'art d'après les Saint-Simoniens,* Paris, Presses Universitaires, 1926.

Weill, Simone, *La France sous la monarchie constitutionelle,* Paris, F. Alcan, 1912.

Wood, John S., *Sondages, 1830-1848, Romanciers français secondaires,* Toronto, University of Toronto Press, 1965.

Wolf, John B., *France 1814-1919, The Rise of a Liberal-Democratic Society,* N. Y., Harper and Row, 1963.

IV. Periodicals

Le Constitutionnel

Gazette de France
Le Globe
Journal des Débats
Journal des Petites Affiches
Revue des Deux Mondes
Revue de Paris et de Saint Pétersbourg
Revue d'Histoire Littéraire de la France

V. Miscellaneous

Fiedler, Leslie A., "Introduction," in George Lippard, *The Monks of Monk Hall,* New York, Odyssey Press, 1970.

Hugo, Victor, *Oeuvres,* Paris, Vve André Houssiaux, 1875.

Kock, Paul de, *Mémoires,* Paris, E. Dentu, 1873.

Pixérécourt, René Charles Guilbert de, *Dernières réflexions sur le mélodrame,* Nancy, 1843.

Sainte Beuve, Charles Auguste, *Chroniques parisiennes, 1843-1845,* Paris, Calmann Lévy, 1876.

Stendhal (Henri Beyle), *Courrier anglais,* Paris, le Divan, 1935.

  Correspondance, 1800-1842, eds. Ad. Paupe, et P. A. Chéramy, Paris, le Divan, 1888, Vol. III.

INDEX

172

174